# KESSINGER PUBLISHING'S
## RARE MYSTICAL REPRINTS

### THOUSANDS OF SCARCE BOOKS
### ON THESE AND OTHER SUBJECTS:

Freemasonry * Akashic * Alchemy * Alternative Health * Ancient Civilizations * Anthroposophy * Astrology * Astronomy * Aura * Bible Study * Cabalah * Cartomancy * Chakras * Clairvoyance * Comparative Religions * Divination * Druids * Eastern Thought * Egyptology * Esoterism * Essenes * Etheric * ESP * Gnosticism * Great White Brotherhood * Hermetics * Kabalah * Karma * Knights Templar * Kundalini * Magic * Meditation * Mediumship * Mesmerism * Metaphysics * Mithraism * Mystery Schools * Mysticism * Mythology * Numerology * Occultism * Palmistry * Pantheism * Parapsychology * Philosophy * Prosperity * Psychokinesis * Psychology * Pyramids * Qabalah * Reincarnation * Rosicrucian * Sacred Geometry * Secret Rituals * Secret Societies * Spiritism * Symbolism * Tarot * Telepathy * Theosophy * Transcendentalism * Upanishads * Vedanta * Wisdom * Yoga * *Plus Much More!*

### DOWNLOAD A FREE CATALOG
### AND
### SEARCH OUR TITLES AT:

### www.kessinger.net

# THE PRACTICE OF
# AUTOSUGGESTION

# THE PRACTICE OF AUTOSUGGESTION

## BY THE METHOD *of* EMILE COUÉ

*Revised Edition*

BY

## C. HARRY BROOKS

WITH A FOREWORD BY
## EMILE COUÉ

"For what man knoweth the things of a man save the spirit of the man which is in him?"

I CORINTHIANS ii. II.

NEW YORK
DODD, MEAD AND COMPANY
1922

COPYRIGHT 1922
BY DODD, MEAD AND COMPANY, INC.

First Printing, May, 1922
Second Printing, June, 1922
Third Printing, June, 1922
Fourth Printing, July, 1922
Fifth Printing, July, 1922
Sixth Printing, Aug., 1922
Seventh Printing, Aug., 1922
Eighth Printing, Aug., 1922
Ninth Printing, Sept., 1922
Tenth Printing, Sept., 1922

PRINTED IN THE U. S. A. BY
The Quinn & Boden Company
BOOK MANUFACTURERS
RAHWAY          NEW JERSEY

TO

ALL IN CONFLICT WITH
THEIR OWN IMPERFECTIONS
THIS LITTLE BOOK
IS DEDICATED

# AUTHOR'S PREFACE

THE discoveries of Emile Coué are of such moment for the happiness and efficiency of the individual life that it is the duty of anyone acquainted with them to pass them on to his fellows.

The lives of many men and women are robbed of their true value by twists and flaws of character and temperament, which, while defying the efforts of the will, would yield rapidly to the influence of autosuggestion. Unfortunately, the knowledge of this method has hitherto been available in England only in the somewhat detailed and technical work of Professor Charles Baudouin, and in a small pamphlet, printed privately by M. Coué, which has not been publicly exposed for sale. To fill this gap is the aim of the following pages. They are designed to present to the layman in non-technical form the information necessary to enable him to practise autosuggestion for himself.

All readers who wish to obtain a deeper insight into the theoretical basis of autosuggestion are recommended to study Professor Baudouin's fascinating work, *Suggestion and Autosuggestion*. Although in these pages there are occasional divergences from Professor Baudouin's views, his book remains beyond question the authoritative statement on the subject; indeed it is hardly possible without it to form an adequate idea of the scope of autosuggestion. My own indebtedness to it in writing this little volume is very great. M. Coué's own pamphlet, *Self-Mastery*, can now be obtained from the Institute for the Practice of Autosuggestion, 20 Grosvenor Gardens, London, S. W. I.

My thanks are due for innumerable kindnesses to M. Coué himself. That he is the embodiment of patience everyone knows who has been in contact with him. I am also indebted to the Rev. Ernest Charles, of Malvern Link, who, though disclaiming responsibility for some of the views expressed here, has made many extremely valuable suggestions.

C. H. B.

Malvern Link,
 *21 February, 1922.*

# FOREWORD

THE materials for this little book were collected by Mr. Brooks during a visit he paid me in the summer of 1921. He was, I think, the first Englishman to come to Nancy with the express purpose of studying my method of conscious autosuggestion. In the course of daily visits extending over some weeks, by attending my consultations, and by private conversations with myself, he obtained a full mastery of the method, and we threshed out a good deal of the theory on which it rests.

The results of this study are contained in the following pages. Mr. Brooks has skilfully seized on the essentials and put them forward in a manner that seems to me both simple and clear. The instructions given are amply sufficient to enable anyone to practise autosuggestion for him or herself, without seeking the help of any other person.

9

It is a method which everyone should follow—the sick to obtain healing, the healthy to prevent the coming of disease in the future.  By its practice we can insure for ourselves, all our lives long, an excellent state of health, both of the mind and the body.

E. COUÉ.

NANCY.

# CONTENTS

## 12   THE PRACTICE OF AUTOSUGGESTION

# I

# COUE'S NANCY PRACTICE

CHAPTER I

## THE CLINIC OF EMILE COUÉ

THE clinic of Emile Coué, where Induced Autosuggestion is applied to the treatment of disease, is situated in a pleasant garden attached to his house at the quiet end of the rue Jeanne d'Arc in Nancy. It was here that I visited him in the early summer of 1921, and had the pleasure for the first time of witnessing one of his consultations.

We entered the garden from his house a little before nine o'clock. In one corner was a brick building of two stories, with its windows thrown wide to let in the air and sunshine—this was the clinic; a few yards away was a smaller one-storied construction which served as a waiting-room. Under the plum and cherry trees, now laden with fruit, little groups of patients were sitting on the garden seats, chatting amicably together and enjoying the morning sunshine while others wandered in twos and threes among the flowers and strawberry beds. The room reserved for the treatments was already crowded, but in spite of that eager newcomers constantly tried to gain entrance. The window-sills on the ground floor were beset, and a dense knot had formed in the doorway. Inside, the patients had first occupied the seats which surrounded the walls, and then covered the available floor-space, sitting on camp-stools and folding-chairs. Coué with some difficulty found me a seat, and the treatment immediately began.

The first patient he addressed was a frail, middle-aged man who, accompanied by his daughter, had just arrived from Paris to consult him. The man was a bad case of nervous trouble. He walked with difficulty, and his head, arms and legs were afflicted with a continual tremor. He explained that if he encountered a stranger when walking in the street the idea that the latter would remark his infirmity completely paralysed him, and he had to cling to whatever support was at hand to save himself from falling. At Coué's invitation he rose from his seat and took a few steps across the floor. He walked slowly, leaning on a stick; his knees were half bent, and his feet dragged heavily along the ground.

Coué encouraged him with the promise of improvement. " You have been sowing bad seed in your Unconscious; now you will sow good seed. The power by which you have produced these ill effects will in future produce equally good ones."

The next patient was an excitable, over-worked woman of the artisan class. When Coué inquired the nature of her trouble, she broke into a flood of complaint, describing each symptom with a voluble minuteness. " Madame," he interrupted, " you think too much about your ailments, and in thinking of them you create fresh ones."

Next came a girl with headaches, a youth with inflamed eyes, and a farm-labourer incapacitated by varicose veins. In each case Coué stated that auto-suggestion should bring complete relief. Then it was the turn of a business man who complained of nervousness, lack of self-confidence and haunting fears.

" When you know the method," said Coué, " you will not allow yourself to harbour such ideas."

"I work terribly hard to get rid of them," the patient answered.

"You fatigue yourself. The greater the efforts you make, the more the ideas return. You will change all that easily, simply, and above all, without effort."

"I want to," the man interjected.

"That's just where you're wrong," Coué told him. "If you say 'I want to do something,' your imagination replies 'Oh, but you can't.' You must say 'I am going to do it,' and if it is in the region of the possible you will succeed."

A little further on was another neurasthenic—a girl. This was her third visit to the clinic, and for ten days she had been practising the method at home. With a happy smile, and a little pardonable self-importance, she declared that she already felt a considerable improvement. She had more energy, was beginning to enjoy life, ate heartily and slept more soundly. Her sincerity and naïve delight helped to strengthen the faith of her fellow-patients. They looked on her as a living proof of the healing which should come to themselves.

Coué continued his questions. Those who were unable, whether through rheumatism or some paralytic affection, to make use of a limb were called on, as a criterion of future progress, to put out their maximum efforts.

In addition to the visitor from Paris there were present a man and a woman who could not walk without support, and a burly peasant, formerly a blacksmith, who for nearly ten years had not succeeded in lifting his right arm above the level of his shoulder. In each case Coué predicted a complete cure.

During this preliminary stage of the treatment, the

words he spoke were not in the nature of suggestions. They were sober expressions of opinion, based on years of experience. Not once did he reject the possibility of cure, though with several patients suffering from organic disease in an advanced stage, he admitted its unlikelihood. To these he promised, however, a cessation of pain, an improvement of morale, and at least a retardment of the progress of the disease. "Meanwhile," he added, "the limits of the power of autosuggestion are not yet known; final recovery is possible." In all cases of functional and nervous disorders, as well as the less serious ones of an organic nature, he stated that autosuggestion, conscientiously applied, was capable of removing the trouble completely.

It took Coué nearly forty minutes to complete his interrogation. Other patients bore witness to the benefits the treatment had already conferred on them. A woman with a painful swelling in her breast, which a doctor had diagnosed (in Coué's opinion wrongly), as of a cancerous nature, had found complete relief after less than three weeks' treatment. Another woman had enriched her impoverished blood, and increased her weight by over nine pounds. A man had been cured of a varicose ulcer, another in a single sitting had rid himself of a lifelong habit of stammering. Only one of the former patients failed to report an improvement. "Monsieur," said Coué, "you have been making efforts. You must put your trust in the imagination, not in the will. Think you are better and you will become so."

Coué now proceeded to outline the theory given in the pages which follow. It is sufficient here to state his main conclusions, which were these: (1) Every idea which exclusively occupies the mind is transformed into an actual physical or mental state. (2) The efforts we make to conquer an idea by exerting the will only serve to make that idea more powerful. To demonstrate these truths he requested one of his patients, a young anæmic-looking woman, to carry out a small experiment. She extended her arms in front of her, and clasped the hands firmly together with the fingers interlaced, increasing the force of her grip until a slight tremor set in. "Look at your hands," said Coué, "and think you would like to open them but you cannot. Now try and pull them apart. Pull hard. You find that the more you try the more tightly they become clasped together."

The girl made little convulsive movements of her wrists, really doing her best by physical force to separate her hands, but the harder she tried the more her grip increased in strength, until the knuckles turned white with the pressure. Her hands seemed locked together by a force outside her own control.

"Now think," said Coué, "'I can open my hands.'"

Slowly her grasp relaxed and, in response to a little pull, the cramped fingers came apart. She smiled shyly at the attention she had attracted, and sat down.

Coué pointed out that the two main points of his theory were thus demonstrated simultaneously: when the patient's mind was filled with the thought "I cannot," she could not in very fact unclasp her hands. Further, the efforts she made to wrench them apart by exerting her will only fixed them more firmly together.

Each patient was now called on in turn to perform the same experiment. The more imaginative among them—notably the women—were at once successful. One old lady was so absorbed in the thought "I can-

not " as not to heed the request to think " I can."
With her face ruefully puckered up she sat staring
fixedly at her interlocked fingers, as though contemplating an act of fate. "Voilà," said Coué, smiling,
" if Madame persists in her present idea, she will never
open her hands again as long as she lives."

Several of the men, however, were not at once successful. The whilom blacksmith with the disabled
arm, when told to think " I should like to open my
hands but I cannot," proceeded without difficulty to
open them.

"You see," said Coué, with a smile, " it depends
not on what I say but on what you think. What were
you thinking then? "

He hesitated. " I thought perhaps I could open
them after all."

" Exactly. And therefore you could. Now clasp
your hands again. Press them together."

When the right degree of pressure had been reached,
Coué told him to repeat the words " I cannot, I cannot. . . ."

As he repeated this phrase the contracture increased,
and all his efforts failed to release his grip.

" Voilà," said Coué. " Now listen. For ten years
you have been thinking you could not lift your arm
above your shoulder, consequently you have not been
able to do so, for whatever we think becomes true
for us. Now think ' I can lift it.' "

The patient looked at him doubtfully.

"Quick!" Coué said in a tone of authority.
" Think ' I can, I can!' "

" I can," said the man. He made a half-hearted
attempt and complained of a pain in his shoulder.

" Bon," said Coué. " Don't lower your arm. Close

your eyes and repeat with me as fast as you can, ' Ca passe, ça passe.' "

For half a minute they repeated this phrase together, speaking so fast as to produce a sound like the whirr of a rapidly revolving machine. Meanwhile Coué quickly stroked the man's shoulder. At the end of that time the patient admitted that his pain had left him.

" Now think well that you can lift your arm," Coué said.

The departure of the pain had given the patient faith. His face, which before had been perplexed and incredulous, brightened as the thought of power took possession of him. " I can," he said in a tone of finality, and without effort he calmly lifted his arm to its full height above his head. He held it there triumphantly for a moment while the whole company applauded and encouraged him.

Coué reached for his hand and shook it.

" My friend, you are cured."

" C'est merveilleux," the man answered. " I believe I am."

" Prove it," said Coué. " Hit me on the shoulder."

The patient laughed, and dealt him a gentle rap.

" Harder," Coué encouraged him. " Hit me harder —as hard as you can."

His arm began to rise and fall in regular blows, increasing in force until Coué was compelled to call on him to stop.

" Voilà, mon ami, you can go back to your anvil."

The man resumed his seat, still hardly able to comprehend what had occurred. Now and then he lifted his arm as if to reassure himself, whispering to himself in an awed voice, " I can, I can."

A little further on was seated a woman who had complained of violent neuralgia. Under the influence of the repeated phrase " ça passe " (it's going) the pain was dispelled in less than thirty seconds. Then it was the turn of the visitor from Paris. What he had seen had inspired him with confidence; he was sitting more erect, there was a little patch of colour in his cheeks, and his trembling seemed less violent.

He performed the experiment with immediate success.

" Now," said Coué, " you are cultivated ground. I can throw out the seed in handfuls."

He caused the sufferer first to stand erect with his back and knees straightened. Then he asked him, constantly thinking " I can," to place his entire weight on each foot in turn, slowly performing the exercise known as " marking time." A space was then cleared of chairs, and having discarded his stick, the man was made to walk to and fro. When his gait became slovenly Coué stopped him, pointed out his fault, and, renewing the thought " I can," caused him to correct it. Progressive improvement kindled the man's imagination. He took himself in his own hands. His bearing became more and more confident, he walked more easily, more quickly. His little daughter, all smiles and happy self-forgetfulness, stood beside him uttering expressions of delight, admiration and encouragement. The whole company laughed and clapped their hands.

" After the sitting," said Coué, " you shall come for a run in my garden."

Thus Coué continued his round of the clinic. Each patient suffering from pain was given complete or partial relief; those with useless limbs had a varying measure of use restored to them. Coué's manner was always quietly inspiring. There was no formality, no attitude of the superior person; he treated everyone, whether rich or poor, with the same friendly solicitude. But within these limits he varied his tone to suit the temperament of the patient. Sometimes he was firm, sometimes gently bantering. He seized every opportunity for a little humorous by-play. One might almost say that he tactfully teased some of his patients, giving them an idea that their ailment was absurd, and a little unworthy; that to be ill was a quaint but reprehensible weakness, which they should quickly get rid of. Indeed, this denial of the dignity of disease is one of the characteristics of the place. No homage is paid to it as a Dread Monarch. It is gently ridiculed, its terrors are made to appear second-rate, and its victims end by laughing at it.

Coué now passed on to the formulation of specific suggestions. The patients closed their eyes, and he proceeded in a low, monotonous voice, to evoke before their minds the states of health, mental and physical, they were seeking. As they listened to him their alertness ebbed away, they were lulled into a drowsy state, peopled only by the vivid images he called up before the eyes of the mind. The faint rustle of the trees, the songs of the birds, the low voices of those waiting in the garden, merged into a pleasant background, on which his words stood out powerfully.

This is what he said:

"Say to yourself that all the words I am about to utter will be fixed, imprinted and engraven in your minds; that they will remain fixed, imprinted and engraven there, so that without your will and knowledge, without your being in any way aware of what is taking place, you yourself and your whole organism will obey them.   I tell you first that every day, three times a day, morning, noon and evening, at mealtimes, you will be hungry; that is to say you will feel that pleasant sensation which makes us think and say: 'How I should like something to eat!'   You will then eat with excellent appetite, enjoying your food, but you will never eat too much.   You will eat the right amount, neither too much nor too little, and you will know intuitively when you have had sufficient.   You will masticate your food thoroughly, transforming it into a smooth paste before swallowing it.   In these conditions you will digest it well, and so feel no discomfort of any kind either in the stomach or the intestines. Assimilation will be perfectly performed, and your organism will make the best possible use of the food to create blood, muscle, strength, energy, in a word— Life.

"Since you have digested your food properly, the excretory functions will be normally performed.   This will take place every morning immediately on rising, and without your having recourse to any laxative medicine or artificial means of any kind.

"Every night you will fall asleep at the hour you wish, and will continue to sleep until the hour at which you desire to wake next morning.   Your sleep will be calm, peaceful and profound, untroubled by bad dreams or undesirable states of body.   You may dream, but your dreams will be pleasant ones.   On waking you will feel well, bright, alert, eager for the day's tasks.

"If in the past you have been subject to depression, gloom and melancholy forebodings, you will henceforward be free from such troubles.   Instead of being moody, anxious and depressed, you will be cheerful

and happy. You will be happy even if you have no
particular reason for being so, just as in the past you
were, without good reason, unhappy. I tell you even
that if you have serious cause to be worried or depressed, you will not be so.

"If you have been impatient or ill-tempered, you
will no longer be anything of the kind; on the contrary,
you will always be patient and self-controlled. The
happenings which used to irritate you will leave you
entirely calm and unmoved.

"If you have sometimes been haunted by evil and
unwholesome ideas, by fears or phobias, these ideas
will gradually cease to occupy your mind. They will
melt away like a cloud. As a dream vanishes when
we wake, so will these vain images disappear.

"I add that all your organs do their work perfectly.
Your heart beats normally and the circulation of the
blood takes place as it should. The lungs do their
work well. The stomach, the intestines, the liver, the
biliary duct, the kidneys and the bladder, all carry out
their functions correctly. If at present any of the organs named is out of order, the disturbance will grow
less day by day, so that within a short space of time
it will have entirely disappeared, and the organ will
have resumed its normal function.

"Further, if in any organ there is a structural lesion,
it will from this day be gradually repaired, and in a
short period will be completely restored. This will be
so even if you are unaware that the trouble exists.

"I must also add—and it is extremely important
—that if in the past you have lacked confidence in yourself, this self-distrust will gradually disappear. You
will have confidence in yourself; I repeat, *you will have
confidence.* Your confidence will be based on the

knowledge of the immense power which is within you, by which you can accomplish any task of which your reason approves. With this confidence you will be able to do anything you wish to do, provided it is reasonable, and anything it is your duty to do.

"When you have any task to perform you will always think that it is easy. Such words as 'difficult,' 'impossible,' 'I cannot' will disappear from your vocabulary. Their place will be taken by this phrase: 'It is easy and I can.' So, considering your work easy, even if it is difficult to others, it will become easy to you. You will do it easily, without effort and without fatigue."

These general suggestions were succeeded by particular suggestions referring to the special ailments from which Coué's patients were suffering. Taking each case in turn, he allowed his hand to rest lightly on the heads of the sufferers, while picturing to their minds the health and vigour with which they would soon be endowed. Thus to a woman with an ulcerated leg he spoke as follows: "Henceforth your organism will do all that is necessary to restore your leg to perfect health. It will rapidly heal; the tissues will regain their tone; the skin will be soft and healthy. In a short space of time your leg will be vigorous and strong and will in future always remain so." Each special complaint was thus treated with a few appropriate phrases. When he had finished, and the patients were called on to open their eyes, a faint sigh went round the room, as if they were awaking reluctantly from a delicious dream.

Coué now explained to his patients that he possessed no healing powers, and had never healed a person in his life. They carried in themselves the instrument

of their own well-being. The results they had seen
were due to the realisation of each patient's own
thought. He had been merely an agent calling the
ideas of health into their minds. Henceforth they
could, and must, be the pilots of their own destiny.
He then requested them to repeat, under conditions
which will be later defined, the phrase with which his
name is associated: " Day by day, in every way, I'm
getting better and better." [1]

The sitting was at an end. The patients rose
and crowded round Coué, asking questions, thanking
him, shaking him by the hand. Some declared they
were already cured, some that they were much better,
others that they were confident of cure in the future.
It was as if a burden of depression had fallen from
their minds. Those who had entered with minds
crushed and oppressed went out with hope and op-
timism shining in their faces.

But Coué waved aside these too insistent admirers,
and, beckoning to the three patients who could not
walk, led them to a corner of the garden where there
was a stretch of gravel path running beneath the
boughs of fruit trees. Once more impressing on their
minds the thought of strength and power, he induced
each one to walk without support down this path.
He now invited them to run. They hesitated, but he
insisted, telling them that they could run, that they
ought to run, that they had but to believe in their own
power, and their thought would be manifested in
action.

They started rather uncertainly, but Coué followed

[1] The translation given here of Coué's formula differs slightly
from that popularised in England during his visit of November,
1921. The above, however, is the English version which he
considers most suitable.

them with persistent encouragements. They began to raise their heads, to lift their feet from the ground and run with greater freedom and confidence. Turning at the end of the path they came back at a fair pace. Their movements were not elegant, but people on the further side of fifty are rarely elegant runners. It was a surprising sight to see these three sufferers who had hobbled to the clinic on sticks now covering the ground at a full five miles an hour, and laughing heartily at themselves as they ran. The crowd of patients who had collected broke into a spontaneous cheer, and Coué, slipping modestly away, returned to the fresh company of sufferers who awaited him within.

CHAPTER II

A FEW OF COUÉ'S CURES

To give the reader a better idea of the results which
Induced Autosuggestion is yielding, I shall here de-
scribe a few further cases of which I was myself in
some part a witness, and thereafter let some of Coué's
patients speak for themselves through the medium of
their letters.

At one of the morning consultations which I sub-
sequently attended was a woman who had suffered
for five years with dyspepsia. The trouble had re-
cently become so acute that even the milk diet to which
she was now reduced caused her extreme discomfort.
Consequently she had become extremely thin and
anæmic, was listless, easily tired, and suffered from
depression. Early in the proceedings the accounts
given by several patients of the relief they had obtained
seemed to appeal to her imagination. She followed
Coué's remarks with keen interest, answered his questions vivaciously, and laughed very heartily at the
amusing incidents with which the proceedings were
interspersed. About five o'clock on the same after-
noon I happened to be sitting with Coué when this
woman asked to see him. Beaming with satisfaction,
she was shown into the room. She reported that on
leaving the clinic she had gone to a restaurant in the
town and ordered a table d'hôte luncheon. Conscientiously she had partaken of every course from the
hors d'œuvres to the café noir. The meal had been

concluded at 1.30, and she had so far experienced no trace of discomfort. A few days later this woman returned to the clinic to report that the dyspepsia had shown no signs of reappearing; that her health and spirits were improving, and that she looked upon herself as cured.

On another occasion one of the patients complained of asthma. The paroxysms destroyed his sleep at night and· prevented him from performing any task which entailed exertion. Walking upstairs was a slow process attended by considerable distress. The experiment with the hands was so successfully performed that Coué assured him of immediate relief.

"Before you go," he said, "you will run up and down those stairs without suffering any inconvenience."

At the close of the consultation, under the influence of the suggestion " I can," the patient did this without difficulty. That night the trouble recurred in a mild form, but he continued to attend the clinic and to practise the exercises at home, and within a fortnight the asthma had finally left him.

Among other patients with whom I conversed was a young man suffering from curvature of the spine. He had been attending the clinic for four months and practising the method at home. His doctor assured him that the spine was gradually resuming its normal position. A girl of twenty-two had suffered from childhood with epileptic fits, recurring at intervals of a few weeks. Since her first visit to the clinic six months previously the fits had ceased.

But the soundest testimony to the power of Induced Autosuggestion is that borne by the patients themselves. Here are a few extracts from letters received by Coué:

" At the age of sixty-three, attacked for more than thirty years by asthma and all the complications attendant upon it, I spent three-quarters of the night sitting on my bed inhaling the smoke of anti-asthma powders. Afflicted with almost daily attacks, especially during the cold and damp seasons, I was unable to walk—I could not even *go down hill.*

Nowadays I have splendid nights, and have put the powders in a drawer. Without the slightest hesitation I can go upstairs to the first floor."

D. (Mont de Marsan.)

15 *December,* 1921.

" Yesterday I felt really better, that is to say, of my fever, so I decided to go back to my doctor, whom I had not seen since the summer. The examination showed a normal appendix. On the other hand, the bladder is still painful, but is better. At any rate, there is at present no question of the operation which had worried me so much. I am convinced that I shall cure myself completely."

M. D. (Mulhouse.)

24 *September,* 1921.

" I have very good news to give you of your dipsomaniac—she is cured, and asserts it herself to all who will listen. She told me yesterday that for fourteen years she had not been so long without drink as she has been lately, and what surprises her so much is that she has not had to struggle against a desire; she has simply not felt the need of drink. Further, her sleep continues to be splendid. She is getting more and more calm, in spite of the fact that on several occasions her sang-froid has been severely tested. To put the matter in a nutshell, she is a changed woman. But what impresses me most is the fact that when she took to your method she thought herself at the end of her tether, and in the event of its doing her no good had decided to kill herself (she had already attempted it once)."

P. (a Paris doctor.)

1 *February,* 1922.

" For eight years I suffered with prolapse of the uterus. I have used your method of Autosuggestion for the last five months, and am now completely cured, for which I do not know how to thank you enough."

S. (Toul).[1]

" I have a son who came back from Germany very anæmic and suffering from terrible depression. He went to see you for a short time, and now is as well as possible. Please accept my best thanks. I have also a little cousin whom you have cured. He had a nervous illness, and had become, so to speak, unconscious of what was going on around him. He is now completely cured."

S. E. (Circourt, Vosges.)

19 *October,* 1921.

" My wife and I have waited nearly a year to thank you for the marvellous cure which your method has accomplished. The very violent attacks of asthma

[1] This letter, together with the two quoted on page 34, is reprinted from the *Bulletin de la Société Lorraine de Psychologie Appliquée* of April, 1921. They were received by Coué during the preceding three months. The other letters were communicated to me privately by Coué and bear their original dates.—

from which my wife suffered have completely disappeared since the visit you paid us last spring. The first few weeks my wife experienced temporary oppression and even the beginnings of an attack, which, however, she was able to ward off within a few minutes by practising Autosuggestion.

In spite of her great desire to thank you sooner my wife wished to add more weight to her testimony by waiting for nearly a year. But the bad time for asthma has not brought the slightest hint of the terrible attacks from which you saved her."

J. H. (Saarbruck.)

*23 December,* 1921.

" All the morbid symptoms from which I used to suffer have disappeared. I used to feel as though I had a band of iron across my brain which seemed to be red-hot; added to this I had heartburn and bad nights with fearful dreams; further, I was subject to severe nervous attacks which went on for months. I felt as though pegs were being driven into the sides of my head and nape of my neck, and when I felt I could not endure these agonies any longer a feeling would come as if my brain were being smothered in a blanket. All these pains came and went. I had sometimes one, sometimes others. There were occasions when I wanted to die—my sufferings were so acute, and I had to struggle against the idea with great firmness.

At last, having spent five weeks at Nancy attending your kindly sittings, I have profited so well as to be able to return home in a state of normal health."

N. (Pithiviviers le Vieil.)

16 *August,* 1921.

"After having undergone four operations on the left leg for local tuberculosis I fell a victim once more to the same trouble on 1 September, 1920. Several doctors whom I consulted declared a new operation necessary. My leg was to be opened from the knee to the ankle, and if the operation failed nothing remained but an amputation.

Having heard of your cures, I came to see you for the first time on 6 November, 1920. After the sitting I felt at once a little better. I followed your instructions exactly, visiting you three times. At the third time I was able to tell you that I was completely cured."

L. (Herny, Lorraine.)

"I am happy to tell you that a bunion that I had on my foot, which grew to a considerable size and gave me the most acute pain for over fifteen years, has gone."

L. G. (Caudéran, Gironde.)

"I cannot leave France without letting you know how grateful I feel for the immense service you have rendered me and mine. I only wish I had met you years ago. Practically throughout my career my curse has been a lack of continuous self-control.

I have been accused of being almost brilliant at times, only to be followed by periodic relapses into a condition of semi-imbecility and self-indulgence.

I have done my best to ruin a magnificent constitution, and have wasted the abilities bestowed upon me. In a few short days you have made me—and I feel permanently—master of myself. How can I thank you sufficiently?

The rapidity of my complete cure may have been due to what at the time I regarded as an unfortunate accident. Slipping on the snow-covered steps of the train when alighting, I sprained my right knee badly. At the breakfast table, before paying you my first visit, a fellow-guest said to me: ' Tell Monsieur Coué about it. He will put it all right.'

I laughed and said ' Umph!' to myself, and more for the fun of the thing than anything else did tell you. I remember you remarking ' That's nothing,' and passing on to the more serious part of our conversation, preliminary to commencing your lecture to the assembled patients.

I became more than interested, and when at the conclusion you suddenly turned round and asked me: ' How's your knee?' (not having alluded to knees in particular), and I discovered there *wasn't* a knee, I laughed again, as did those who saw me hobble into your room; but I laughed this time from a sense of bewildered surprise and dawning belief. This belief you very soon firmly implanted in me."

G. H. (London.)

11 *January,* 1922.

## CHAPTER III

## THE CHILDREN'S CLINIC

IN different parts of France a little band of workers, recruited almost exclusively from the ranks of former patients, is propagating the ideas of Emile Coué with a success which almost rivals that of their master. Among these helpers none is more devoted or more eminently successful than Mlle. Kauffmant. She it is who, at the time of my visit, was managing the children's department of the Nancy clinic.[1]

While Coué was holding his consultations on the ground floor, young mothers in twos and threes, with their babies in their arms, could be seen ascending to the upper story, where a little drama was performed of a very different nature from that going on below.

In a large room, decorated with bright pictures and equipped with toys, a number of silent young women were seated in a wide circle. Their sick children lay in their arms or played at their feet. Here was a child whose life was choked at the source by hereditary disease—a small bundle of skin and bone with limbs like bamboo canes. Another lay motionless with closed eyes and a deathly face, as if pining to return to the world it came from. A little cripple dragged behind it a deformed leg as it tried to crawl, and near by a child of five was beating the air with its thin arms in an exhausting nervous storm. Older children were also present, suffering from eye and ear trouble, epilepsy, rickets, any one of the ailments, grave or slight, to which growing life is subjected.

1 Since this time (July, 1921), the clinic has been in some respects reorganized and Mlle. Kauffmant is now pursuing her work independently.

36

In the centre of this circle sat a young woman with dark hair and a kindly keen face. On her lap was a little boy of four years with a club foot. As she gently caressed the foot, from which the clumsy boot had been removed, she told in a crooning tone, mingled with endearing phrases, of the rapid improvement which had already begun and would soon be complete. The foot was getting better; the joints were more supple and bent with greater ease; the muscles were developing, the tendons were drawing the foot into the right shape and making it straight and strong. Soon it would be perfectly normal; the little one would walk and run, play with other children, skip and bowl hoops. He would go to school and learn his lessons, would be intelligent and receptive. She told him too that he was growing obedient, cheerful, kind to others, truthful and courageous. The little boy had put one arm round her neck and was listening with a placid smile. His face was quite contented; he was enjoying himself.

While Mlle. Kauffmant was thus engaged, the women sat silent watching her intently, each perhaps mentally seeing her own little one endowed with the qualities depicted. The children were quiet, some dreamily listening, some tranquilly playing with a toy. Except for an occasional word of advice Mademoiselle was quite indifferent to them. Her whole attention was given to the child on her knee; her thought went out to him in a continual stream, borne along by a current of love and compassion, for she has devoted her life to the children and loves them as if they were her own. The atmosphere of the room was more like that of a church than a hospital. The mothers seemed to have left their sorrows outside. Their faces showed in varying degrees an expression of quiet confidence.

When this treatment had continued for about ten minutes, Mlle. Kauffmant returned the child to its mother and, after giving her a few words of advice, turned to her next patient. This was an infant of less than twelve months. While suffering from no specific disease it was continually ailing. It was below normal weight, various foods had been tried unsuccessfully, and medical advice had failed to bring about an improvement. Mademoiselle resumed her seat with the child on her lap. For some time the caresses, which were applied to the child's head and body, continued in silence. Then she began to talk to it. Her talk did not consist of connected sentences, as with the elder child who had learned to speak, but of murmured assurances, as if her thoughts were taking unconsciously the form of words. These suggestions were more general than in the previous case, bearing on appetite, digestion, assimilation, and on desirable mental and moral qualities. The caress continued for about ten minutes, the speech was intermittent, then the infant was returned to its mother and Mademoiselle turned her attention to another little sufferer.

With patients who are not yet old enough to speak Mlle. Kauffmant sometimes trusts to the caress alone. It seems to transmit the thoughts of health quite strongly enough to turn the balance in the child's mind on the side of health. But all mothers talk to their children long before the words they use are understood, and Mlle. Kauffmant, whose attitude is essentially maternal, reserves to herself the same right. She adheres to no rigid rule; if she wishes to speak aloud she does so, even when the child cannot grasp the meaning of her words.

This is perhaps the secret of her success: her method

is plastic like the minds she works on. Coué's material—the adult mind—is more stable. It demands a clear-cut, distinct method, and leaves less room for adaptation; but the aim of Mlle. Kauffmant is to fill the child within and enwrap it without with the creative thoughts of health and joy. To this end she enlists any and every means within her power. The child itself, as soon as it is old enough to speak, is required to say, morning and night, the general formula: " Day by day, in every way, I'm getting better and better." If it is confined to its bed, it is encouraged to repeat this at any time and to make suggestions of health similar to those formulated in the sittings. No special directions are given as to how this should be done. Elaborate instructions would only introduce hindersome complications. Imagination, the power to pretend, is naturally strong and active in all children, and intuitively they make use of it in their autosuggestions. Moreover, they unconsciously imitate the tone and manner of their instructress.

But the centre of the child's universe is the mother. Any system which did not utilise her influence would be losing its most powerful ally. The mother is encouraged during the day to set an example of cheerfulness and confidence, to allude to the malady only in terms of encouragement—so renewing in the child's mind the prospect of recovery—and to exclude as far as possible all depressing influences from its vicinity. At night she is required to enter the child's bedchamber without waking the little one and to whisper good suggestions into its sleeping ear. Thus Mlle. Kauffmant concentrates a multiplicity of means to bring about the same result. In this she is aided by the extreme acceptivity of the child's mind, and by the absence of that mass of pernicious spontaneous suggestions which in the adult mind have to be neutralised and transformed. It is in children, then, that the most encouraging results may be expected. I will quote three cases which I myself investigated to show the kind of results Mlle. Kauffmant obtains:

A little girl was born without the power of sight. The visual organs were intact, but she was incapable of lifting her eye-lids and so remained blind to all intents and purposes up to her seventh year. She was then brought by the mother to Mlle. Kauffmant. After a fortnight's treatment the child began to blink; gradually this action became more frequent, and a month after the treatment began she could see well enough to find her way unaided about the streets. When I saw her she had learnt to distinguish colours—as my own experiments proved—and was actually playing ball. The details supplied by Mlle. Kauffmant were confirmed by the mother.

A child was born whose tuberculous father had died during the mother's pregnancy. Of five brothers and sisters none had survived the first year. The doctors to whom the child was taken held out no hope for its life. It survived, however, to the age of two, but was crippled and nearly blind, in addition to internal weaknesses. It was then brought to Mlle. Kauffmant. Three months later, when I saw it, nothing remained of its troubles but a slight squint and a stiffness in one of its knee-joints. These conditions, too, were rapidly diminishing.

Another child, about nine years of age, also of tuberculous parents, was placed under her treatment. One leg was an inch and a half shorter than the other. After a few months' treatment this disparity had almost disappeared. The same child had a wound, also of tuberculous origin, on the small of the back, which healed over in a few weeks and had completely disappeared when I saw her.

In each of the above cases the general state of health showed a great improvement. The child put on weight, was cheerful and bright even under the trying conditions of convalescence in a poverty-stricken home, and in character and disposition fully realised the suggestions formulated to it.

Since the suggestions of Mlle. Kauffmant are applied individually, the mothers were permitted to enter and leave the clinic at any time they wished. Mademoiselle was present on certain days every week, but this was not the sum of her labours. The greater part of her spare time was spent in visiting the little ones in their own homes. She penetrated into the dingiest tenements, the poorest slums, on this errand of mercy. I was able to accompany her on several of these visits, and saw her everywhere received not only with welcome, but with a respect akin to awe. She was regarded, almost as much as Coué himself, as a worker of miracles. But the reputation of both Coué and Mlle. Kauffmant rests on a broader basis even than autosuggestion, namely on their great goodness of heart.

They have placed not only their private means, but their whole life at the service of others. Neither ever accepts a penny-piece for the treatments they give, and I have never seen Coué refuse to give a treatment at however awkward an hour the subject may have asked it. The fame of the school has now spread to all parts not only of France, but of Europe and America. Coué's work has assumed such proportions that his time is taken up often to the extent of fifteen or sixteen hours a day. He is now nearing his seventieth year, but thanks to the health-giving powers of his own method he is able to keep abreast of his work without any sign of fatigue and without the clouding of his habitual cheerfulness by even the shadow of a complaint. In fact, he is a living monument to the efficacy of Induced Autosuggestion.

It will be seen that Induced Autosuggestion is a method by which the mind can act directly upon itself and upon the body to produce whatever improvements, in reason, we desire. That it is efficient and successful should be manifest from what has gone before. Of all the questions which arise, the most urgent from the viewpoint of the average man seems to be this —Is a suggester necessary? Must one submit oneself to the influence of some other person, or can one in the privacy of one's own chamber exercise with equal success this potent instrument of health?

Coué's own opinion has already been quoted. Induced Autosuggestion is *not* dependent upon the mediation of another person. We can practise it for ourselves without others being even aware of what we are doing, and without devoting to it more than a few minutes of each day.

Here are a few quotations from letters written by those who have thus practised it for themselves.

" For a good many years now a rheumatic right shoulder has made it impossible for me to sleep on my right side and it seriously affected, and increasingly so, the use of my right arm. A masseuse told me she could effect no permanent improvement as there was granulation of the joints and a lesion. I suddenly realised two days ago that this shoulder no longer troubled me and that I was sleeping on that side without any pain. I have now lost any sensation of rheumatism in this shoulder and can get my right arm back as far as the other without the slightest twinge or discomfort. I have not applied any remedy or done anything that could possibly have worked these results except my practise of Coué."

L. S. (Sidmouth, Devon).

1 *January, 1922.*

" At my suggestion a lady friend of mine who had been ill for a good ten years read *La Maîtrise de soi-meme*. I encouraged her as well as I could, and in a month she was transformed. Her husband, returning from a long journey, could not believe his eyes. This woman who never got up till midday, who never left the fire-side, whom the doctors had given up, now goes out at 10 a.m. even in the greatest cold. Other friends are anxiously waiting to read your pamphlet.

L. C. (Paris).

17 *December, 1921.*

" I am very much interested in your method, and since your lecture I have, every night and morning, repeated your little phrase. I used to have to take a pill every night, but now my constipation is cured and the pills are no longer necessary. My wife is also much better in every way. We've both got the bit of string with twenty knots."

H. (a London doctor).

7 *January, 1922.*

" Your method is doing me more good every day. I don't know how to thank you for the happiness I now experience. I shall never give up repeating the little phrase."

E. B. Guiévain (Belgium).

*23 November, 1921.*


" I have followed your principles for several months and freed myself from a terrible state of neurasthenia which was the despair of my three doctors."

G. (Angoulême).

*23 January, 1922.*


" My friend Miss C. completely cured herself of a rheumatic shoulder and knee in a very short time, and then proceeded to turn her attention to her eyesight.

She had worn spectacles for 30 years and her left eye was much more short-sighted than her right. When she began she could only read (without her glasses and with her left eye) when the book was almost touching her face. In six weeks she had extended the limit of vision so that she saw as far with the left as formerly with the right. Meanwhile the right had improved equally. She measured the distances every week, and when she was here a few days ago she told me she had in three days gained 4 centimetres with her left and 6 centimetres with her right eye. She had done this on her own."

G. (London).

*5 January, 1922.*

# II

# THE NATURE OF AUTOSUGGESTION

CHAPTER IV

## THOUGHT IS A FORCE

AUTOSUGGESTION is not a pseudo-religion like Christian Science or "New Thought." It is a scientific method based on the discoveries of psychology. The traditional psychology was regarded by the layman, not without some cause, as a dull and seemingly useless classification of our conscious faculties. But within the past twenty-five years the science has undergone a great change. A revolution has taken place in it which seems likely to provoke a revolution equally profound in the wider limits of our common life. From a preoccupation with the conscious it has turned to the Unconscious (or subconscious), to the vast area of mental activity which exists outside the circle of our awareness. In doing so it has grasped at the very roots of life itself, has groped down to the depths where the "life-force," the élan vital, touches our individual being. What this may entail in the future we can only dimly guess. Just as the discovery of America altered the balance of the Old World, shifting it westward to the shores of the Atlantic, so the discovery and investigation of the Unconscious seems destined to shift the balance of human life.

Obviously, this is no place to embark on the discussion of a subject of such extreme complexity. The investigation of the Unconscious is a science in itself, in which different schools of thought are seeking to disengage a basis of fact from conflicting and daily changing theories.   But there is a certain body of fact, experimentally proven, on which the authorities agree, and of this we quote a few features which directly interest us as students of autosuggestion.

The Unconscious is the storehouse of memory, where every impression we receive from earliest infancy to the last hour of life is recorded with the minutest accuracy.   These memories, however, are not inert and quiescent, like the marks on the vulcanite records of a gramophone; they are vitally active, each one forming a thread in the texture of our personality.   The sum of all these impressions is the man himself, the ego, the form through which the general life is individualised.   The outer man is but a mask; the real self dwells behind the veil of the Unconscious.

The Unconscious is also a power-house.   It is dominated by feeling, and feeling is the force which impels our lives.   It provides the energy for conscious thought and action, and for the performance of the vital processes of the body.

Finally the Unconscious plays the part of supervisor over our physical processes.   Digestion, assimilation, the circulation of the blood, the action of the lungs, the kidneys and all the vital organs are controlled by its agency.   Our organism is not a clockwork machine which once wound up will run of itself.   Its processes in all their complexity are supervised by mind.   It is not the intellect, however, which does this work, but the Unconscious.   The intellect still stands aghast before the problem of the human body, lost like Pascal in the profundities of analysis, each discovery only revealing new depths of mystery.   But the Unconscious seems to be familiar with it in every detail.

It may be added that the Unconscious never sleeps;

during the sleep of the conscious it seems to be more vigilant than during our waking hours.

In comparison with these, the powers of the conscious mind seem almost insignificant. Derived from the Unconscious during the process of evolution, the conscious is, as it were, the antechamber where the crude energies of the Unconscious are selected and adapted for action on the world outside us. In the past we have unduly exaggerated the importance of the conscious intellect. To claim for it the discoveries of civilisation is to confuse the instrument with the agent, to attribute sight to the field-glass instead of to the eye behind it. The value of the conscious mind must not be underrated, however. It is a machine of the greatest value, the seat of reason, the social instincts and moral concepts. But it *is* a machine and not the engine, nor yet the engineer. It provides neither material nor power. These are furnished by the Unconscious.

These two strata of mental life are in perpetual interaction one with the other. Just as everything conscious has its preliminary step in the Unconscious, so every conscious thought passes down into the lower stratum and there becomes an element in our being, partaking of the Unconscious energy, and playing its part in supervising and determining our mental and bodily states. If it is a healthful thought we are so much the better; if it is a diseased one we are so much the worse. It is this transformation of a thought into an element of our life that we call Autosuggestion. Since this is a normal part of the mind's action we shall have no difficulty in finding evidence of it in our daily experiences.

Walking down the street in a gloomy frame of mind

you meet a buoyant, cheery acquaintance. The mere sight of his genial smile acts on you like a tonic, and when you have chatted with him for a few minutes your gloom has disappeared, giving place to cheerfulness and confidence. What has effected this change? —Nothing other than the idea in your own mind. As you watched his face, listened to his good-natured voice, noticed the play of his smile, your conscious mind was occupied by the idea of cheerfulness. This idea on being transferred to the Unconscious became a reality, so that without any logical grounds you became cheerful.

Few people, especially young people, are unacquainted with the effects produced by hearing or reading ghost-stories. You have spent the evening, let us say, at a friend's house, listening to terrifying tales of apparitions. At a late hour you leave the fireside circle to make your way home. The states of fear imaged before your mind have realised themselves in your Unconscious. You tread gingerly in the dark places, hurry past the churchyard and feel a distinct relief when the lights of home come into view. It is the old road you have so often traversed with perfect equanimity, but its cheerful associations are overlooked and the commonest objects tinged with the colour of your subjective states. Autosuggestion cannot change a post into a spectre, but if you are very impressionable it will so distort your sensory impressions that common sounds seem charged with supernatural significance and every-day objects take on terrifying shapes.

In each of the above examples the idea of a mental state—cheerfulness or fear—was presented to the mind. The idea on reaching the Unconscious became a reality; that is to say, you actually became cheerful or frightened.

The same process is much easier to recognise where the resultant is not a mental but a bodily state.

One often meets people who take a delight in describing with a wealth of detail the disorders with which they or their friends are afflicted. A sensitive person is condemned by social usage to listen to a harrowing account of some grave malady. As detail succeeds detail the listener feels a chilly discomfort stealing over him. He turns pale, breaks into a cold perspiration, and is aware of an unpleasant sensation at the pit of the stomach. Sometimes, generally where the listener is a child, actual vomiting or a fainting fit may ensue. These effects are undeniably physical; to produce them the organic processes must have been sensibly disturbed. Yet their cause lies entirely in the idea of illness, which, ruthlessly impressed upon the mind, realises itself in the Unconscious.

This effect may be so precise as to reproduce the actual symptoms of the disease described. Medical students engaged in the study of some particular malady frequently develop its characteristic symptoms.

Everyone is acquainted with the experience known as " stage fright." The victim may be a normal person, healthy both in mind and body. He may possess in private life a good voice, a mind fertile in ideas and a gift of fluent expression. He may know quite surely that his audience is friendly and sympathetic to the ideas he wishes to unfold. But let him mount the steps of a platform. Immediately his knees begin to tremble and his heart to palpitate; his mind becomes a blank or a chaos, his tongue and lips refuse to frame coherent sounds, and after a few stammerings he is forced to make a ludicrous withdrawal. The cause of this baffling experience lay in the thoughts which occupied the subject's mind before his public appearance. He was afraid of making himself ridiculous. He expected to feel uncomfortable, feared that he would forget his speech or be unable to express himself. These negative ideas, penetrating to the Unconscious, realised themselves and precisely what he feared took place.

If you live in a town you have probably seen people who, in carelessly crossing the street, find themselves in danger of being run down by a vehicle. In this position they sometimes stand for an appreciable time "rooted," as we say, "to the spot." This is because the danger seems so close that they imagine themselves powerless to elude it. As soon as this idea gives place to that of escape they get out of the way as fast as they can. If their first idea persisted, however, the actual powerlessness resulting from it would likewise persist, and unless the vehicle stopped or turned aside they would infallibly be run over.

One occasionally meets people suffering from a nervous complaint known as St. Vitus' Dance. They have a disconcerting habit of contorting their faces, screwing round their necks or twitching their shoulders. It is a well known fact that those who come into close contact with them, living in the same house or working in the same office, are liable to contract the same habit, often performing the action without themselves being aware of it. This is due to the operation of the same law. The idea of the habit, being repeatedly presented to their minds, realises itself, and they begin to perform a similar movement in their own persons.

Examples of this law present themselves at every turn. Have you ever asked yourself why some people faint at the sight of blood, or why most of us turn giddy when we look down from a great height?

If we turn to the sufferers from neurosis we find some who have lost their powers of speech or of vision; some, like the blacksmith we saw in Coué's clinic, who have lost the use of their limbs; others suffering from a functional disturbance of one of the vital organs. The cause in each case is nothing more tangible than an idea which has become realised in the Unconscious mind.

These instances show clearly enough that the thoughts we think do actually become realities in the Unconscious. But is this a universal law, operating in every life, or merely something contingent and occasional? Sometimes irrelevant cheerfulness seems only to make despondency more deep. Certain types of individual are only irritated by the performance of a stage comedy. Physicians listen to the circumstantial accounts of their patients' ailments without being in the least upset. These facts seem at first sight at variance with the rule. But they are only apparent exceptions which serve to test and verify it. The physical or mental effect invariably corresponds with the idea present in the mind, but this need not be identical with the thought communicated from without. Sometimes a judgment interposes itself, or it may be that the idea calls up an associated idea which possesses greater vitality and therefore dislodges it. A gloomy person who meets a cheerful acquaintance may mentally contrast himself with the latter, setting his own troubles beside the other's good fortune, his own grounds for sadness beside the other's grounds for satisfaction. Thus the idea of his own unhappiness is strengthened and sinking into the Unconscious makes still deeper the despondency he experienced before. In the same way the doctor, listening to the symptoms of a patient, does not allow these distressful ideas to dwell in his conscious mind. His thought passes on immediately to the remedy, to the idea of the help he must give. Not only does he manifest this helpfulness in reasoned action, but also, by Unconscious realisation, in his very bearing and manner. Or his mind may be concentrated on the scientific bearings of the case, so that he will involuntarily treat the patient as a specimen on which to pursue his researches. The steeplejack experiences no giddiness or fear in scaling a church spire because the thought of danger is immediately replaced by the knowledge of his own clear head and sure foot.

This brings us to a point which is of great practical importance in the performance of curative autosuggestion. No idea presented to the mind can realise itself unless the mind accepts it.

Most of the errors made hitherto in this field have been due to the neglect of this fundamental fact. If a patient is suffering from severe toothache it is not of the slightest use to say to him: " You have no pain." The statement is so grossly opposed to the fact that " acceptation " is impossible. The patient will reject the suggestion, affirm the fact of his suffering, and so, by allowing his conscious mind to dwell on it, probably make it more intense.

We are now in a position to formulate the basic law of autosuggestion as follows :—

*Every idea which enters the conscious mind, if it is accepted by the Unconscious, is transformed by it into a reality and forms henceforth a permanent element in our life.*

This is the process called "Spontaneous Autosuggestion." It is a law by which the mind of man has always worked, and by which all our minds are working daily.

The reader will see from the examples cited and from others which he will constantly meet that the thoughts we think determine not only our mental states, our sentiments and emotions, but the delicate actions and adjustments of our physical bodies. Trembling, palpitation, stammering, blushing—not to speak of the pathological states which occur in neurosis— are due to modifications and changes in the blood-flow, in muscular action and in the working of the vital organs. These changes are not voluntary and conscious ones, they are determined by the Unconscious and come to us often with a shock of surprise.

It must be evident that if we fill our conscious minds with ideas of health, joy, goodness, efficiency, and can ensure their acceptation by the Unconscious, these ideas too will become realities, capable of lifting us on to a new plane of being. The difficulty which has hitherto so frequently brought these hopes to naught is that of ensuring acceptation. This will be treated in the next chapter.

To sum up, the whole process of Autosuggestion consists of two steps: (1) The acceptation of an idea. (2) Its transformation into a reality. Both these operations are performed by the Unconscious. Whether the idea is originated in the mind of the subject or is presented from without by the agency of another person is a matter of indifference. In both cases it undergoes the same process: it is submitted to the Unconscious, accepted or rejected, and so either realised or ignored. Thus the distinction between Autosuggestion and Heterosuggestion is seen to be both arbitrary and superficial. In essentials all suggestion is Autosuggestion. The only distinction we need make is between Spontaneous Autosuggestion, which takes place independently of our will and choice, and Induced Autosuggestion, in which we consciously select the ideas we wish to realise and purposely convey them to the Unconscious.

## CHAPTER V

## THOUGHT AND THE WILL

IF we can get the Unconscious to accept an idea, realisation follows automatically. The only difficulty which
confronts us in the practice of Induced Autosuggestion
is to ensure acceptation, and that is a difficulty which
no method prior to that of Emile Coué has satisfac-
torily surmounted.

Every idea which enters the mind is charged, to a
greater or less extent, with emotion. This emotional
charge may be imperceptible, as with ideas to which
we are indifferent, or it may be very great, as when
the idea is closely related to our personal interests.
All the ideas we are likely to make the subjects of
Induced Autosuggestion are of the latter class, since
they refer to health, energy, success or some goal
equally dear to our hearts. The greater the degree of
emotion accompanying an idea, the more potent is the
autosuggestion resulting from it. Thus a moment of
violent fright may give rise to effects which last a
lifetime. This emotional factor also plays a large part
in securing acceptation.

So far as one can see, the acceptation or rejection
of an idea by the Unconscious depends on the associations with which it is connected. Thus, an idea is
accepted when it evokes similar ideas charged with
emotion of the same quality. It is rejected when it is
associated with contrary ideas, which are, therefore,
contrary in their emotional charge. In the latter case,

the original idea is neutralised by its associations, somewhat in the same way as an acid is neutralised by an alkali. An example will serve to make this clearer.

You are on a cross-channel boat on a roughish passage. You go up to a sailor and say to him in a sympathetic tone: " My dear fellow, you're looking very ill. Aren't you going to be sea-sick? " According to his temperament he either laughs at your " joke " or expresses a pardonable irritation. But he does not become sick because the associations called up are contrary ones. Sea-sickness is associated in his mind with his own immunity from it, and therefore evokes not fear but self-confidence. Pursuing your somewhat inhumane experiment you approach a timid-looking passenger. " My dear sir, how ill you look! I feel sure you are going to be sea-sick. Let me help you down below." He turns pale. The word " sea-sickness " associates itself with his own fears and forebodings. He accepts your aid down to his berth and there the pernicious autosuggestion is realised. In the first case the idea was refused, because it was overwhelmed by a contrary association; in the second the Unconscious accepted it, since it was reinforced by similar ideas from within.

But supposing to a sick mind, permeated with thoughts of disease, a thought of health is presented. How can we avoid the malassociation which tends to neutralise it?

We can think of the Unconscious as a tide which ebbs and flows. In sleep it seems to submerge the conscious altogether, while at our moments of full wakefulness, when the attention and will are both at work, the tide is at its lowest ebb. Between these two extremes are any number of intermediary levels. When we are drowsy, dreamy, lulled into a gentle reverie by music or by a picture or a poem, the Unconscious tide is high; the more wakeful and alert we become the lower it sinks. This submersion of the conscious mind is called by Baudouin the "Outcropping of the Subconscious." The highest degree of outcropping, compatible with the conscious direction of our thoughts, occurs just before we fall asleep and just after we wake.

It is fairly obvious that the greater the outcropping the more accessible these dynamic strata of the mind become, and the easier it is to implant there any idea we wish to realise.

As the Unconscious tide rises the active levels of the mind are overflowed; thought is released from its task of serving our conscious aims in the real world of matter, and moves among the more primal wishes and desires which people the Unconscious, like a diver walking the strange world beneath the sea. But the laws by which thought is governed on this sub-surface level are not those of our ordinary waking consciousness. During outcropping association by contraries does not seem readily to take place. Thus the mal-association, which neutralised the desired idea and so prevented acceptation, no longer presents itself. We all know what happens during a "day-dream" or "brown-study," when the Unconscious tide is high. A succession of bright images glides smoothly through the mind. The original thought spins itself on and on; no obstacles seem to stop it, no questions of probability arise; we are cut off from the actual conditions of life and live in a world where all things are possible. These day-dreams cause very potent autosuggestions, and one should take care that they are wholesome and innocent; but the important point is that on this level of consciousness association seems to operate by similarity, and emotion is comparatively intense. These conditions are highly favourable to acceptation.

If, on getting into bed at night, we assume a comfortable posture, relax our muscles and close our eyes, we fall naturally into a stage of semi-consciousness akin to that of day-dreaming. If now we introduce into the mind any desired idea, it is freed from the inhibiting associations of daily life, associates itself by similarity, and attracts emotion of the same quality as its own charge. The Unconscious is thus caused to accept it, and inevitably it is turned into an auto-suggestion. Every time we repeat this process the associative power of the idea is increased, its emotional value grows greater, and the autosuggestion resulting from it is more powerful. By this means we can induce the Unconscious to accept an idea, the normal associations of which are contrary and unfavourable. The person with a disease-soaked mind can gradually implant ideas of health, filling his Unconscious daily with healing thoughts. The instrument we use is Thought, and the condition essential to success is that the conscious mind shall be lulled to rest.

Systems which hitherto have tried to make use of autosuggestion have failed to secure reliable results because they did not place their reliance on Thought, but tried to compel the Unconscious to accept an idea by exercising the Will. Obviously, such attempts are doomed to failure. By using the will we automatically wake ourselves up, suppress the encroaching tide of the Unconscious, and thereby destroy the condition by which alone we can succeed.

It is worth our while to note more closely how this

happens. A sufferer, whose mind is filled with thoughts of ill-health, sits down to compel himself to accept a good suggestion. He calls up a thought of health and makes an effort of the will to impress it on the Unconscious. This effort restores him to full wakefulness and so evokes the customary association —disease. Consequently, he finds himself contemplating the exact opposite of what he desired. He summons his will again and recalls the healthful thought, but since he is now wider awake than ever, association is even more rapid and powerful than before. The disease-thought is now in full possession of his mind and all the efforts of his will fail to dislodge it. Indeed the harder he struggles the more fully the evil thought possesses him.

This gives us a glimpse of the new and startling discovery to which Coué's uniform success is due; namely, that when the will is in conflict with an idea, the idea invariably gains the day. This is true, of course, not only of Induced Autosuggestion, but also of the spontaneous suggestions which occur in daily life. A few examples will make this clear.

Most of us know how, when we have some difficult duty to perform, a chance word of discouragement will dwell in the mind, eating away our self-confidence and attuning our minds to failure. All the efforts of our will fail to throw it off; indeed, the more we struggle against it the more we become obsessed with it.

Very similar to this is the state of mind of the person suffering from stage-fright. He is obsessed with ideas of failure and all the efforts of his will are powerless to overcome them. Indeed, it is the state of effort and tension which makes his discomfiture so complete.

Sport offers many examples of the working of this law.

A tennis-player is engaged to play in an important match. He wishes, of course, to win, but fears that he will lose. Even before the day of the game his fears begin to realise themselves. He is nervy and "out of sorts." In fact, the Unconscious is creating the conditions best suited to realise the thought in his mind—failure. When the game begins his skill seems to have deserted him. He summons the resources of his will and tries to compel himself to play well, straining every nerve to recapture the old dexterity. But all his efforts only make him play worse and worse. The harder he tries the more signally he fails. The energy he calls up obeys not his will but the idea in his mind, not the desire to win but the dominant thought of failure.

The fatal attraction of the bunker for the nervous golfer is due to the same cause. With his mind's eye he sees his ball alighting in the most unfavourable spot. He may use any club he likes, he may make a long drive or a short; as long as the thought of the bunker dominates his mind, the ball will inevitably find its way into it. The more he calls on his will to help him, the worse his plight is likely to be. Success is not gained by effort but by right thinking. The champion golfer or tennis-player is not a person of herculean frame and immense will-power. His whole life has been dominated by the thought of success in the game at which he excels.

Young persons sitting for an examination sometimes undergo this painful experience. On reading through their papers they find that all their knowledge has suddenly deserted them. Their mind is an appalling blank and not one relevant thought can they recall. The more they grit their teeth and summon the powers of the will, the further the desired ideas flee. But when they have left the examination-room and the tension relaxes, the ideas they were seeking flow tantalisingly back into the mind. Their forgetfulness was due to thoughts of failure previously nourished in the mind. The application of the will only made the disaster more complete.

This explains the baffling experience of the drug-taker, the drunkard, the victim of some vicious craving. His mind is obsessed by the desire for satisfaction. The efforts of the will to restrain it only make it more overmastering. Repeated failures convince him at length that he is powerless to control himself, and this idea, operating as an auto-suggestion, increases his impotence. So in despair, he abandons himself to his obsession, and his life ends in wreckage.

We can now see, not only that the Will is incapable of vanquishing a thought, but that as fast as the Will brings up its big guns, Thought captures them and turns them against it.

This truth, which Baudouin calls the Law of Reversed Effort, is thus stated by Coué:

*"When the Imagination and the Will are in conflict the Imagination invariably gains the day."*

*"In the conflict between the Will and the Imagination, the force of the Imagination is in direct ratio to the square of the Will."*

The mathematical terms are used, of course, only metaphorically.

Thus the Will turns out to be, not the commanding monarch of life, as many people would have it, but a blind Samson, capable either of turning the mill or of pulling down the pillars.

Autosuggestion succeeds by avoiding conflict. It replaces wrong thought by right, literally applying in the sphere of science the principle enunciated in the New Testament: " Resist not evil, but overcome evil with good."

This doctrine is in no sense a negation of the will. It simply puts it in its right place, subordinates it to a higher power. A moment's reflection will suffice to show that the will cannot be more than the servant of thought. We are incapable of exercising the will unless the imagination has first furnished it with a goal. We cannot simply will, we must will *something*, and that something exists in our minds as an idea. The will acts rightly when it is in harmony with the idea in the mind.

But what happens when, in the smooth execution of our idea, we are confronted with an obstacle? This obstacle may exist outside us, as did the golfer's bunker, but it must also exist as an idea in our minds or we should not be aware of it.

As long as we allow this mental image to stay there, the efforts of our will to overcome it only make it more irresistible. We run our heads against it like a goat butting a brick wall. Indeed, in this way we can magnify the smallest difficulty until it becomes insurmountable—we can make mole-hills into mountains. This is precisely what the neurasthenic does. The idea of a difficulty dwells unchanged in his mind, and all his efforts to overcome it only increase its dimensions, until it overpowers him and he faints in the effort to cross a street.

But as soon as we change the idea our troubles

vanish. By means of the intellect we can substitute for the blank idea of the obstacle that of the means to overcome it. Immediately, the will is brought into harmony again with thought, and we go forward to the triumphant attainment of our end. It may be that the means adopted consist of a frontal attack, the overcoming of an obstacle by force. But before we bring this force into play, the mind must have approved it—must have entertained the idea of its probable success. We must, in fact, have thought of the obstacle as already smashed down and flattened out by our attack. Otherwise, we should involve ourselves in the conflict depicted above, and our force would be exhausted in a futile internal battle. In a frontal attack against an obstacle we use effort, and effort, to be effective, must be approved by the reason and preceded, to some extent, by the idea of success.

Thus, even in our dealings with the outside world, Thought is always master of the will. How much more so when our action is turned inward! When practising autosuggestion we are living in the mind, where thoughts are the only realities. We can meet with no obstacle other than that of Thought itself. Obviously then, the frontal attack, the exertion of effort, can never be admissible, for it sets the will and the thought at once in opposition. The turning of our thoughts from the mere recognition of an obstacle to the idea of the means to overcome it, is no longer a preliminary, as in the case of outward action. In itself it clears away the obstacle. By procuring the right idea our end is already attained.

In applying effort during the practice of Induced Autosuggestion, we use in the world of mind an instrument fashioned for use in the world of matter. It is as if we tried to solve a mathematical problem by mauling the book with a tin-opener.

For two reasons then, effort must never be allowed to intrude during the practice of autosuggestion: first because it wakes us up and so suppresses the tide of the Unconscious, secondly because it causes conflict between Thought and the will.

One other interesting fact emerges from an examination of the foregoing examples. In each case we find that the idea which occupied the mind was of a final state, an accomplished fact. The golfer was thinking of his ball dropping into the bunker, the tennis-player of his defeat, the examinee of his failure. In each case the Unconscious realised the thought in its own way, chose inevitably the means best suited to arrive at its end—the realisation of the idea. In the case of the golfer the most delicate physical adjustments were necessary. Stance, grip and swing all contributed their quota, but these physical adjustments were performed unconsciously, the conscious mind being unaware of them. From this we see that we need not suggest the way in which our aim is to be accomplished. If we fill our minds with the thought of the desired end, provided that end is possible, the Unconscious will lead us to it by the easiest, most direct path.

Here we catch a glimpse of the truth behind what is called "luck." We are told that everything comes to him who waits, and this is literally true, provided he waits in the right frame of mind. Some men are notoriously lucky in business; whatever they touch seems to "turn to gold." The secret of their success lies in the fact that they confidently expect to succeed.

There is no need to go so far as the writers of the school of " New Thought," and claim that suggestion can set in motion transcendental laws outside man's own nature. It is quite clear that the man who expects success, of whatever kind it may be, will unconsciously take up the right attitude to his environment; will involuntarily close with fleeting opportunity, and by his inner fitness command the circumstances without.

Man has often been likened to a ship navigating the seas of life. Of that ship the engine is the will and Thought is the helm. If we are being directed out of our true course it is worse than useless to call for full steam ahead; our only hope lies in changing the direction of the helm.

# III

# THE PRACTICE OF AUTOSUGGESTION

## CHAPTER VI

## GENERAL RULES

WITH our knowledge of the powerful effect which an idea produces, we shall see the importance of exercising a more careful censorship over the thoughts which enter our minds. Thought is the legislative power in our lives, just as the will is the executive. We should not think it wise to permit the inmates of prisons and asylums to occupy the legislative posts in the state, yet when we harbour ideas of passion and disease, we allow the criminals and lunatics of thought to usurp the governing power in the commonwealth of our being.

In future, then, we shall seek ideas of health, success, and goodness; we shall treat warily all depressing subjects of conversation, the daily list of crimes and disasters which fill the newspapers, and those novels, plays and films which harrow our feelings, without transmuting by the magic of art the sadness into beauty.

This does not mean that we should be always self-consciously studying ourselves, ready to nip the pernicious idea in the bud; nor yet that we should adopt the ostrich's policy of sticking our heads in the sand and declaring that disease and evil have no real existence. The one leads to egotism and the other to callousness. Duty sometimes requires us to give our attention to things in themselves evil and depressing. The demands of friendship and human sympathy are imperious, and we cannot ignore them without moral loss. But there is a positive and a negative way of approaching such subjects.

Sympathy is too often regarded as a passive process by which we allow ourselves to be infected by the gloom, the weakness, the mental ill-health of other people. This is sympathy perverted. If a friend is suffering from small-pox or scarlet fever you do not seek to prove your sympathy by infecting yourself with his disease. You would recognize this to be a crime against the community. Yet many people submit themselves to infection by unhealthy ideas as if it were an act of charity—part of their duty towards their neighbours. In the same way people deliver their minds to harrowing stories of famine and pestilence, as if the mental depression thus produced were of some value to the far-away victims. This is obviously false—the only result is to cause gloom and ill-health in the reader and so make him a burden to his family. That such disasters should be known is beyond question, but we should react to them in the manner indicated in the last chapter. We should replace the blank recognition of the evil by the quest of the means best suited to overcome it; then we can look forward to an inspiring end and place the powers of our will in the service of its attainment.

> Oh, human soul, as long as thou canst so,
> Set up a mark of everlasting light
> Above the heaving senses' ebb and flow . . .
> Not with lost toil thou labourest through the night,
> Thou mak'st the heaven thou hop'st indeed thy home.

Autosuggestion, far from producing callousness, dictates the method and supplies the means by which the truest sympathy can be practised. In every case our aim must be to remove the suffering as soon as possible, and this is facilitated by refusing acceptation to the bad ideas and maintaining our own mental and moral balance.

Whenever gloomy thoughts come to us, whether from without or within, we should quietly transfer our attention to something brighter. Even if we are afflicted by some actual malady, we should keep our thought from resting on it as far as we have the power to do so. An organic disease may be increased a hundredfold by allowing the mind to brood on it, for in so doing we place at its disposal all the resources of our organism, and direct our life-force to our own destruction. On the other hand, by denying it our attention and opposing it with curative autosuggestions, we reduce its power to the minimum and should succeed in overcoming it entirely. Even in the most serious organic diseases the element contributed by wrong thought is infinitely greater than that which is purely physical.

There are times when temperamental failings, or the gravity of our affliction, places our imagination beyond our ordinary control. The suggestion operates in spite of us; we do not seem to possess the power to rid our minds of the adverse thought. Under these conditions we should never struggle to throw off the obsessing idea by force. Our exertions only bring into play the law of reversed effort, and we flounder deeper into the slough. Coué's technique, however, which will be outlined in succeeding chapters, will give us the means of mastering ourselves, even under the most trying conditions.

Of all the destructive suggestions we must learn to shun, none is more dangerous than fear. In fearing something the mind is not only dwelling on a negative idea, but it is establishing the closest personal connection between the idea and ourselves. Moreover, the idea is surrounded by an aura of emotion, which considerably intensifies its effect. Fear combines every element necessary to give to an autosuggestion its maximum power. But happily fear, too, is susceptible to the controlling power of autosuggestion. It is one of the first things which a person cognisant of the means to be applied should seek to eradicate from his mind.

For our own sakes, too, we should avoid dwelling on the faults and frailties of our neighbours. If ideas of selfishness, greed, vanity, are continually before our minds there is great danger that we shall subconsciously accept them, and so realise them in our own character. The petty gossip and backbiting, so common in a small town, produce the very faults they seem to condemn. But by allowing our minds to rest upon the virtues of our neighbours, we reproduce the same virtues in ourselves.

But if we should avoid negative ideas for our own sakes, much more should we do so for the sake of other people. Gloomy and despondent men and women are centres of mental contagion, damaging all with whom they come in contact. Sometimes such people seem involuntarily to exert themselves to quench the cheerfulness of brighter natures, as if their Unconscious strove to reduce all others to its own low level. But even healthy, well-intentioned people scatter evil suggestions broadcast, without the least suspicion of the harm they do. Every time we remark to an acquaintance that he is looking ill, we actually damage his health; the effect may be extremely slight, but by repetition it grows powerful. A man who accepts in the course of a day fifteen or twenty suggestions that he is ill, has gone a considerable part of the way towards actual illness. Similarly, when we thoughtlessly commiserate with a friend on the difficulty of his daily work, or represent it as irksome and uncongenial, we make it a little harder for him to accomplish, and thereby slightly diminish his chances of success.

If we must supervise our speech in contact with adults, with children we should exercise still greater foresight. The child's Unconscious is far more accessible than that of the adult; the selective power exercised by the conscious mind is much feebler, and consequently the impressions received realise themselves with greater power. These impressions are the material from which the child's growing life is constructed, and if we supply faulty material the resultant structure will be unstable. Yet the most attentive and well-meaning mothers are engaged daily in sowing the seeds of weakness in their children's minds. The little ones are constantly told they will take cold, will be sick, will fall down, or will suffer some other misfortune. The more delicate the child's health, the more likely it is to be subjected to adverse suggestions. It is too often saturated with the idea of bad health, and comes to look on disease as the normal state of existence and health as exceptional. The same is equally true of the child's mental and moral upbringing. How often do foolish parents tell their children that they are naughty, disobedient, stupid, idle or vicious? If these suggestions were accepted, which, thank Heaven, is not always the case, the little ones would in very fact develop just these qualities. But even when no word is spoken, a look or a gesture can initiate an undesirable autosuggestion. The same child, visited by two strangers, will immediately make friends with the one and avoid the other. Why is this?—Because the one carries with him a healthful atmosphere, while the other sends out waves of irritability or gloom.

" Men imagine," says Emerson, " that they communicate their virtue or vice only by overt actions, and do not see that virtue and vice emit a breath every moment."

With children, above all, it is not sufficient to refrain from the expression of negative ideas; we must avoid harbouring them altogether. Unless we possess a bright positive mind the suggestions derived from us will be of little value.

The idea is gaining ground that a great deal of what is called hereditary disease is transmitted from parent to child, not physically but mentally—that is to say, by means of adverse suggestions continually renewed in the child's mind. Thus if one of the parents has a tendency to tuberculosis, the child often lives in an atmosphere laden with tuberculous thoughts. The little one is continually advised to take care of its lungs, to keep its chest warm, to beware of colds, etc., etc. In other words, the idea is repeatedly presented to its mind that it possesses second-rate lungs. The realisation of these ideas, the actual production of pulmonary tuberculosis is thus almost assured.

But all this is no more than crystallised commonsense. Everyone knows that a cheerful mind suffuses health, while a gloomy one produces conditions favourable to disease. " A merry heart doeth good like a medicine," says the writer of the Book of Proverbs,.

"but a broken spirit drieth the bones." But this knowledge, since it lacked a scientific basis, has never been systematically applied. We have regarded our feelings far too much as *effects* and not sufficiently as *causes*. We are happy because we are well; we do not recognise that the process will work equally well in the reverse direction—that we shall be well because we are happy. Happiness is not only the result of our conditions of life; it is also the creator of those conditions. Autosuggestion lays weight upon this latter view. Happiness must come first. It is only when the mind is ordered, balanced, filled with the light of sweet and joyous thought, that it can work with its maximum efficiency. When we are habitually happy our powers and capabilities come to their full blossom, and we are able to work with the utmost effect on the shaping of what lies without.

Happiness, you say, cannot be ordered like a chop in a restaurant. Like love, its very essence is freedom. This is true; but like love, it can be wooed and won. It is a condition which everyone experiences at some time in life. It is native to the mind. By the systematic practice of Induced Autosuggestion we can make it, not a fleeting visitant, but a regular tenant of the mind, which storms and stresses from without cannot dislodge. This idea of the indwelling happiness, inwardly conditioned, is as ancient as thought. By autosuggestion we can realise it in our own lives.

## CHAPTER VII

## THE GENERAL FORMULA

WE saw that an unskilled golfer, who imagines his ball is going to alight in a bunker, unconsciously performs just those physical movements needful to realise his idea in the actual. In realising this idea his Unconscious displays ingenuity and skill none the less admirable because opposed to his desire. From this and other examples we concluded that if the mind dwells on the idea of an accomplished fact, a realised state, the Unconscious will produce this state. If this is true of our spontaneous autosuggestions it is equally true of the self-induced ones.

It follows that if we consistently think of happiness we become happy; if we think of health we become healthy; if we think of goodness we become good. Whatever thought we continually think, provided it is reasonable, tends to become an actual condition of our life.

Traditionally we rely too much on the conscious mind. If a man suffers from headaches he searches out, with the help of his physician, their cause; discovers whether they come from his eyes, his digestion or his nerves, and purchases the drugs best suited to repair the fault. If he wishes to improve a bad memory he practises one of the various methods of memory-training. If he is the victim of a pernicious habit he is left to counter it by efforts of the will, which too often exhaust his strength, undermine his self-respect, and only lead him deeper into the mire. How simple in comparison is the method of Induced Autosuggestion! He need merely think the end—a head free from pain, a good memory, a mode of life in which his bad habit has no part, and these states are gradually evolved without his being aware of the operation performed by the Unconscious.

But even so, if each individual difficulty required a fresh treatment—one for the headache, one for the memory, one for the bad habit and so on—then the time needful to practise autosuggestion would form a considerable part of our waking life. Happily the researches of the Nancy School have revealed a further simplification. This is obtained by the use of a general formula which sets before the mind the idea of a daily improvement in every respect, mental, physical and moral.

In the original French this formula runs as follows: "Tous les jours, à tous points de vue, je vais de mieux en mieux." The English version which Coué considers most satisfactory is this: "*Day by day, in every way, I'm getting better and better.*" This is very easy to say, the youngest child can understand it, and it possesses a rudimentary rhythm, which exerts a lulling effect on the mind and so aids in calling up the Unconscious. But if you are accustomed to any other version, such as that recommended by the translators of Baudouin, it would be better to continue to use it. Religious minds who wish to associate the formula with God's care and protection might do so after this fashion: "Day by day, in every way, by the help of God, I'm getting better and better." It is possible that the attention of the Unconscious will thus be turned to moral and spiritual improvements to a greater extent than by the ordinary formula.

But this general formula possesses definite advantages other than mere terseness and convenience. The Unconscious, in its character of surveyor over our mental and physical functions, knows far better than the conscious the precise failings and weaknesses which have the greatest need of attention. The general formula supplies it with a fund of healing, strengthening power, and leaves it to apply this at the points where the need is most urgent.

It is a matter of common experience that people's ideals of manhood and womanhood vary considerably. The hardened materialist pictures perfection solely in terms of wealth, the butterfly-woman wants little but physical beauty, charm, and the qualities that attract. The sensitive man is apt to depreciate the powers he possesses and exaggerate those he lacks; while his self-satisfied neighbour can see no good in any virtues but his own. It is quite conceivable that a person left free to determine the nature of his autosuggestions by the light of his conscious desire might use this power to realise a quality not in itself admirable, or even one which, judged by higher standards, appeared pernicious. Even supposing that his choice was good he would be in danger of over-developing a few characteristics to the detriment of others and so destroying the balance of his personality. The use of the general formula guards against this. It saves a man in spite of himself. It avoids the pitfalls into which the conscious mind may lead us by appealing to a more competent authority. Just as we leave the distribution of our bodily food to the choice of the Unconscious, so we may safely leave that of our mental food, our Induced Autosuggestions.

The fear that the universal use of this formula would have a standardising effect, modifying its users to a uniform pattern, is unfounded. A rigid system of particular suggestions might tend towards such a result, but the general formula leaves every mind free to unfold and develop in the manner most natural to itself. The eternal diversity of men's minds can only be increased by the free impulse thus administered.

We have previously seen that the Unconscious tide rises to its highest point compatible with conscious thought just before sleep and just after awaking, and that the suggestions formulated then are almost assured acceptation. It is these moments that we select for the repetition of the formula.

But before we pass on to the precise method, a word of warning is necessary. Even the most superficial attempt to analyse intellectually a living act is bound to make it appear complex and difficult. So our consideration of the processes of outcropping and acceptation has inevitably invested them with a false appearance of difficulty. Autosuggestion is above all things easy. Its greatest enemy is effort. The more simple and unforced the manner of its performance the more potently and profoundly it works. This is shown by the fact that its most remarkable results have been secured by children and by simple French peasants.

It is here that Coué's directions for the practice differ considerably from those of Baudouin. Coué insists upon its easiness, Baudouin complicates it. The four chapters devoted by the latter to " relaxation," " collection," " contention," and " concentration," produce in the reader an adverse suggestion of no mean power. They leave the impression that autosuggestion is a perplexing business which only the greatest foresight and supervision can render successful. Nothing could be more calculated to throw the beginner off the track.

We have seen that Autosuggestion is a function of the mind which we spontaneously perform every day of our lives. The more our induced autosuggestions approximate to this spontaneous prototype the more potent they are likely to be. Baudouin warns us against the danger of setting the intellect to do the work of intuition, yet this is precisely what he himself does. A patient trying by his rules to attain outcropping and implant therein an autosuggestion is so vigilantly attentive to what he is doing that outcropping is rendered almost impossible. These artificial aids are, in Coué's opinion, not only unnecessary but hindersome. Autosuggestion succeeds when Conscious and Unconscious co-operate in the acceptance of an idea. Coué's long practice has shown that we must leave the Unconscious, as senior partner in the concern, to bring about the right conditions in its own way. The fussy attempts of the intellect to dictate the method of processes which lie outside its sphere will only produce conflict, and so condemn our attempt to failure. The directions given here are amply sufficient, if conscientiously applied, to secure the fullest benefits of which the method is capable.

Take a piece of string and tie in it twenty knots. By this means you can count with a minimum expenditure of attention, as a devout Catholic counts his prayers on a rosary. The number twenty has no intrinsic virtue; it is merely adopted as a suitable round number.

On getting into bed close your eyes, relax your muscles and take up a comfortable posture. These are no more than the ordinary preliminaries of slumber. Now repeat twenty times, counting by means of the knots, the general formula: " Day by day, in every way, I'm getting better and better."

The words should be uttered aloud; that is, loud enough to be audible to your own ears. In this way the idea is reinforced by the movements of lips and tongue and by the auditory impressions conveyed through the ear. Say it simply, without effort, like a child absently murmuring a nursery rhyme. Thus you avoid an appeal to the critical faculties of the conscious which would lessen the outcropping. When you have got used to this exercise and can say it quite " unself-consciously," begin to let your voice rise or fall— it does not matter which—on the phrase " in every way." This is perhaps the most important part of the formula, and is thus given a gentle emphasis. But at first do not attempt this accentuation; it will only needlessly complicate and, by requiring more conscious attention, may introduce effort. Do not try to think of what you are saying. On the contrary, let the mind wander whither it will; if it rests on the formula all the better, if it strays elsewhere do not recall it. As long as your repetition does not come to a full-stop your mind-wandering will be less disturbing than would be the effort to recall your thoughts.

Baudouin differs from Coué as to the manner in which the formula should be repeated. His advice is to say it " piously," with all the words separately stressed. No doubt it has its value when thus spoken, but the attitude of mind to which the word " pious " can be applied is unfortunately not habitual with everyone. The average man in trying to be " pious " might end by being merely artificial. But the child still exists in the most mature of men. The " infantile " mode of repeating the formula puts one in touch with deep levels of the Unconscious where the child-mind still survives. Coué's remarkable successes have been obtained by this means, and Baudouin advances no cogent reason for changing it.

These instructions no doubt fall somewhat short of our ideal of a thought entirely occupying the mind. But they are sufficient for a beginning. The sovereign rule is to make no effort, and if this is observed you will intuitively fall into the right attitude. This process of Unconscious adaptation may be hastened by a simple suggestion before beginning. Say to yourself, " I shall repeat the formula in such a manner as to secure its maximum effect." This will bring about the required conditions much more effectively than any conscious exercise of thought.

On waking in the morning, before you rise, repeat the formula in exactly the same manner.

Its regular repetition is the foundation stone of the Nancy method and should never be neglected. In times of health it may be regarded as an envoy going before to clear the path of whatever evils may lurk in the future. But we must look on it chiefly as an educator, as a means of leavening the mass of adverse spontaneous suggestions which clog the Unconscious and rob our lives of their true significance.

Say it with faith. When you have said it your conscious part of the process is completed. Leave the Unconscious to do its work undisturbed. Do not be anxious about it, continually scanning yourself for signs of improvement. The farmer does not turn over the clods every morning to see if his seed is sprouting. Once sown it is left till the green blade appears. So it should be with suggestion. Sow the seed, and be sure the Unconscious powers of the mind will bring it to fruition, and all the sooner if your conscious ego is content to let it rest.

*Say it with faith!* You can only rob Induced Autosuggestion of its power in one way—by believing that it is powerless. If you believe this it becomes ipso facto powerless for you. The greater your faith the more radical and the more rapid will be your results; though if you have only sufficient faith to repeat the formula twenty times night and morning the results will soon give you in your own person the proof you desire, and facts and faith will go on mutually augmenting each other.

Faith reposes on reason and must have its grounds. What grounds can we adduce for faith in Induced Autosuggestion? The examples of cures already cited are outside your experience and you may be tempted to pooh-pooh them. The experiment of Chevreul's pendulum, however, will show in a simple manner the power possessed by a thought to transform itself into an action.

Take a piece of white paper and draw on it a circle of about five inches' radius. Draw two diameters *A B* and *C D* at right angles to each other and intersecting at *O*. The more distinctly the lines stand out the better—they should be thickly drawn in black ink. Now take a lead pencil or a light ruler and tie to one end a piece of cotton about eight inches long; to the lower end of the cotton fasten a heavy metal button, of the sort used on a soldier's tunic. Place the paper on a table so that the diameter $A B$ seems to be horizontal and $C D$ to be vertical, thus:

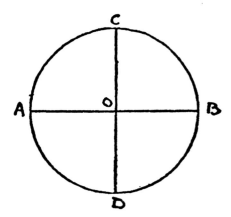

Stand upright before the table with your miniature fishing-rod held firmly in both hands and the button suspended above the point $O$. Take care not to press the elbows nervously against the sides.

Look at the line $A B$, think of it, follow it with your eyes from side to side. Presently the button will begin to swing along the line you are thinking of. The more your mind dwells easily upon the idea of the line the greater this swing becomes. Your efforts to *try* to hold the pendulum still, by bringing into action the law of reversed effort, only make its oscillations more pronounced.

Now fix your eyes on the line $C D$. The button will gradually change the direction of its movement, taking up that of $C D$. When you have allowed it to swing thus for a few moments transfer your attention to the circle, follow the circumference round and round with your eyes. Once more the swinging button will follow you, adopting either a clock-wise or a counter clock-wise direction according to your thought. After a little practice you should produce a circular swing with a diameter of at least eight inches; but your success will be directly proportional to the exclusiveness of your thought and to your efforts to hold the pencil still.

Lastly think of the point *O*. Gradually the radius of the swing will diminish until the button comes to rest.

Is it necessary to point out how these movements are caused? Your thought of the line, passing into the Unconscious, is there realised, so that *without knowing it* you execute with your hands the imperceptible movements which set the button in motion. The Unconscious automatically realises your thought through the nerves and muscles of your arms and hands. What is this but Induced Autosuggestion?

The first time you perform this little experiment it is best to be alone. This enables you to approach it quite objectively.

## CHAPTER VIII

## PARTICULAR SUGGESTIONS

THE use of particular suggestions outlined in this chapter is of minor importance compared with that of the general formula—" Day by day, in every way, I'm getting better and better." The more deeply Coué pursues his investigations, the more fully he becomes convinced that all else is secondary to this. It is not difficult to make a guess as to why this should be. In the general formula the attention is fully absorbed by the idea of betterment. The mind is directed away from all that hinders and impedes and fixed on a positive goal. In formulating particular suggestions, however, we are always skating on the thin ice round our faults and ailments, always touching on subjects which have the most painful associations. So that our ideas have not the same creative positiveness. However that may be, it is a matter of experience that the general formula is the basis of the whole method, and that all else is merely an adjuvant, an auxiliary—useful, but inessential to the main object.

We have seen that a partial outcropping of the Unconscious takes place whenever we relax our mental and physical control, and let the mind wander; in popular language, when we fall into a " brown study " or a " day-dream." This outcropping should be sought before the special suggestions are formulated.

But again we must beware of making simple things seem hard. Baudouin would have us perform a num-

88

ber of elaborate preparatives, which, however valuable to the student of psychology, serve with the layman only to distract the mind, and by fixing the attention on the mechanism impair the power of the creative idea. Moreover, they cause the subject to exert efforts to attain a state the very essence of which is effortlessness, like the victim of insomnia who " tries his hardest " to fall asleep.

In order to formulate particular suggestions, go to a room where you will be free from interruption, sit down in a comfortable chair, close your eyes, and let your muscles relax. In other words, act precisely as if you were going to take a siesta. In doing so you allow the Unconscious tide to rise to a sufficient height to make your particular suggestions effective. Now call up the desired ideas through the medium of speech. Tell yourself that such and such ameliorations are going to occur.

But here we must give a few hints as to the *form* these suggestions should take.

We should never set our faith a greater task than it can accomplish. A patient suffering from deafness would be ill-advised to make the suggestion: " I can hear perfectly." In the partial state of outcropping association is not entirely cut off, and such an idea would certainly call up its contrary. Thus we should initiate a suggestion antagonistic to the one we desired. In this way we only court disappointment and by losing faith in our instrument rob it of its efficacy.

Further, we should avoid as far as possible all mention of the ailment or difficulty against which the suggestion is aimed. Indeed, our own attention should be directed not so much to getting rid of wrong conditions as to cultivating the opposite right ones in their place. If you are inclined to be neurasthenic your mind is frequently occupied with fear. This fear haunts you because some thwarted element in your personality, surviving in the Unconscious, gains through it a perverse satisfaction. In other words, your Unconscious enjoys the morbid emotional condition which fear brings with it. Should you succeed in banishing your fears you would probably feel dissatisfied, life would seem empty. The old ideas would beckon you with promises, not of happiness truly, but of emotion and excitement. But if your suggestions take a positive form, if you fill your mind with thoughts of self-confidence, courage, outward activity, and interest in the glowing and vital things of life, the morbid ideas will be turned out of doors and there will be no vacant spot to which they can return.

Whatever the disorder may be, we should refer to it as little as possible, letting the whole attention go out to the contrary state of health. We must dwell on the " Yes-idea," affirming with faith the realisation of our hopes, seeing ourselves endowed with the triumphant qualities we lack. For a similar reason we should never employ a form of words which connotes doubt. The phrases, " I should like to," " I am going to try," if realised by the Unconscious, can only produce a state of longing or desire, very different from the actual physical and mental modifications we are seeking.

Finally, we should not speak of the desired improvement entirely as a thing of the future. We should affirm that the change has already begun, and will continue to operate more and more rapidly until our end is fully attained.

Here are a few examples of special suggestions which may prove useful.

For deafness: Having closed the eyes and relaxed body and mind, say to yourself something of this nature: " From this day forth my hearing will gradually improve. Each day I shall hear a little better. Gradually this improvement will become more and more rapid until, in a comparatively short space of time, I shall hear quite well and I shall continue to do so until the end of my life."

A person suffering from unfounded fears and forebodings might proceed as follows: " From to-day onward I shall become more and more conscious of all that is happy, positive and cheerful. The thoughts which enter my mind will be strong and healthful ones. I shall gain daily in self-confidence, shall believe in my own powers, which indeed at the same time will manifest themselves in greater strength. My life is growing smoother, easier, brighter. These changes become from day to day more profound; in a short space of time I shall have risen to a new plane of life, and all the troubles which used to perplex me will have vanished and will never return."

A bad memory might be treated in some such terms as these: " My memory from to-day on will improve in every department. The impressions received will be clearer and more definite; I shall retain them automatically and without any effort on my part, and when I wish to recall them they will immediately present themselves in their correct form to my mind. This improvement will be accomplished rapidly, and very soon my memory will be better than it has ever been before."

Irritability and bad temper are very susceptible to

autosuggestion and might be thus treated: "Henceforth I shall daily grow more good-humoured. Equanimity and cheerfulness will become my normal states of mind, and in a short time all the little happenings of life will be received in this spirit. I shall be a centre of cheer and helpfulness to those about me, infecting them with my own good humour, and this cheerful mood will become so habitual that nothing can rob me of it."

Asthma is a disease which has always baffled and still baffles the ordinary methods of medicine. It has shown itself, however, in Coué's experience, pre-eminently susceptible to autosuggestive treatment. Particular suggestions for its removal might take this form: "From this day forward my breathing will become rapidly easier. Quite without my knowledge, and without any effort on my part, my organism will do all that is necessary to restore perfect health to my lungs and bronchial passages. I shall be able to undergo any exertion without inconvenience. My breathing will be free, deep, delightful. I shall draw in all the pure health-giving air I need, and thus my whole system will be invigorated and strengthened. Moreover, I shall sleep calmly and peacefully, with the maximum of refreshment and repose, so that I awake cheerful and looking forward with pleasure to the day's tasks. This process has this day begun and in a short time I shall be wholly and permanently restored to health."

It will be noticed that each of these suggestions comprises three stages: (1) Immediate commencement of the amelioration. (2) Rapid progress. (3) Complete and permanent cure. While this scheme is not essential, it is a convenient one and should be utilised whenever applicable. The examples are framed as the first autosuggestions of persons new to the method. On succeeding occasions the phrase " from this day forth," or its variants, should be replaced by a statement that the amelioration has already begun. Thus, in the case of the asthmatic, " My breathing is already becoming easier," etc.

Particular suggestions, though subsidiary in value to the general formula, are at times of very great service. The general formula looks after the foundations of our life, building in the depths where eye cannot see or ear hear. Particular suggestions are useful on the surface. By their means we can deal with individual difficulties as they arise. The two methods are complementary.

Particular suggestions prove very valuable in reinforcing and rendering permanent the effects obtained by the technique for overcoming pain, which will be outlined in the next chapter. Before commencing the attack we should sit down, close our eyes and say calmly and confidently to ourselves: " I am now going to rid myself of this pain." When the desired result has been obtained, we should suggest that the state of ease and painlessness now re-established will be permanent, that the affected part will rapidly be toned up into a condition of normal health, and will remain always in that desirable state. Should we have obtained only a lessening of the trouble without its complete removal our suggestion should take this form: "I have obtained a considerable degree of relief, and in the next few minutes it will become complete. I shall be restored to my normal condition of health and shall continue so for the future." Thus our assault upon the pain is made under the best conditions, and should in every case prove successful.

We should employ particular suggestions also for overcoming the difficulties which confront us from time to time in our daily lives, and for securing the full success of any task we take in hand. The use of the general suggestion will gradually strengthen our self-confidence, until we shall expect success in any enterprise of which the reason approves. But until this consummation is reached, until our balance of self-confidence is adequate for all our needs, we can obtain an overdraft for immediate use by means of particular suggestion.

We have already seen that the dimensions of any obstacle depend at least as much upon our mental attitude towards it as upon its intrinsic difficulty. The neurasthenic, who imagines he cannot rise from his bed, cannot do so because this simple operation is endowed by his mind with immense difficulty. The great mass of normal people commit the same fault in a less degree. Their energy is expended partly in doing their daily work, and partly in overcoming the resistance in their own minds. By the action of the law of reversed effort the negative idea they foster frequently brings their efforts to naught, and the very exertions they make condemn their activities to failure.

For this reason it is necessary, before undertaking any task which seems to us difficult, to suggest that it is in fact easy. We close our eyes and say quietly to ourselves, " The work I have to do is easy, quite easy. Since it is easy I can do it, and I shall do it efficiently and successfully. Moreover, I shall enjoy doing it; it will give me pleasure, my whole personality will apply itself harmoniously to the task, and the results will be even beyond my expectation." We should dwell on these ideas, repeating them tranquilly and effortlessly. Soon our mind will become serene, full of hope and confidence. Then we can begin to think out our method of procedure, to let the mind dwell on the means best suited to attain our object. Since the impediments created by fear and anxiety are now removed our ideas will flow freely, our plans will construct themselves in the quiet of the mind, and we shall come to the actual work with a creative vigour and singleness of purpose.

By a similar procedure the problems of conduct which defy solution by conscious thought will frequently yield to autosuggestion. When we are " at our wits' ends," as the saying goes, to discover the best path out of a dilemma, when choice between conflicting possibilities seems impossible, it is worse than useless to continue the struggle. The law of reversed effort is at work paralysing our mental faculties. We should put it aside, let the waves of effort subside, and suggest to ourselves that at a particular point of time the solution will come to us of its own accord. If we can conveniently do so, it is well to let a period of sleep intervene, to suggest that the solution will come to us on the morrow; for during sleep the Unconscious is left undisturbed to realise in its own way the end we have consciously set before it.

This operation often takes place spontaneously, as when a problem left unsolved the night before yields its solution apparently by an inspiration when we arise in the morning. " Sleep on it " still remains the best counsel for those in perplexity, but they should preface their slumbers by the positive autosuggestion that on waking they will find the difficulty resolved. In this connection it is interesting to note that autosuggestion is already widely made use of as a means of waking at a particular hour. A person who falls asleep with the idea in his mind of the time at which he wishes to wake, will wake at that time. It may be added that wherever sleep is utilised for the realisation of particular suggestions, these suggestions should be made in addition to the general formula, either immediately before or immediately after; they should never be substituted for it.

With some afflictions, such as fits, the attack is often so sudden and unexpected that the patient is smitten down before he has a chance to defend himself. Particular suggestions should be aimed first of all at securing due warning of the approaching attack. We should employ such terms as these: " In future I shall always know well in advance when a fit is coming on. I shall be amply warned of its approach. When these warnings occur I shall feel no fear or anxiety. I shall be quite confident of my power to avert it." As soon as the warning comes—as it will come, quite unmistakably—the sufferer should isolate himself and use a particular suggestion to prevent the fit from developing. He should first suggest calm and self-control, then affirm repeatedly, but of course without effort, that the normal state of health is re-asserting itself, that the mind is fully under control, and that nothing can disturb its balance. All sudden paroxysms, liable to take us unexpectedly, should be treated by the same method, which in Coué's experience has amply justified itself.

Nervous troubles and violent emotions, such as fear and anger, often express themselves by physical movements. Fear may cause trembling, palpitation, chattering of the teeth; anger a violent clenching of the fists. Baudouin advises that particular suggestions in these cases should be directed rather against the motor expression than against the psychic cause, that our aim should be to cultivate a state of physical impassibility. But since a positive suggestion possesses greater force than a negative, it would seem better to attack simultaneously both the cause and the effect. Instead of anger, suggest that you will feel sympathy, patience, good-humour, and consequently that your bodily state will be easy and unconstrained.

A form of particular suggestion which possesses distinct advantages of its own is the quiet repetition of a single word. If your mind is distracted and confused, sit down, close your eyes, and murmur slowly and reflectively the single word " Calm." Say it reverently, drawing it out to its full length and pausing after each repetition. Gradually your mind will be stilled and quietened, and you will be filled with a sense of harmony and peace. This method seems most applicable to the attainment of moral qualities. An evil passion can be quelled by the use of the word denoting the contrary virtue. The power of the word depends largely upon its æsthetic and moral associations. Words like joy, strength, love, purity, denoting the highest ideals of the human mind, possess great potency and are capable, thus used, of dispelling mental states in which their opposites predominate. The name Reflective Suggestion, which Baudouin applies indifferently to all autosuggestions induced by the subject's own choice, might well be reserved for this specific form of particular suggestion.

The field for the exercise of particular suggestions

is practically limitless.   Whenever you feel a need for betterment, of whatever nature it may be, a particular suggestion will help you.   But it must once more be repeated that these particular suggestions are merely aids and auxiliaries, which may, if leisure is scant, be neglected.

## CHAPTER IX

## HOW TO DEAL WITH PAIN

PAIN, whether of mind or body, introduces a new element for which we have hitherto made no provision. By monopolising the attention it keeps the conscious mind fully alert and so prevents one from attaining the measure of outcropping needful to initiate successfully an autosuggestion. Thus if we introduce the "no-pain" idea into the conscious, it is overwhelmed by its contrary—pain, and the patient's condition becomes, if anything, worse.

To overcome this difficulty quite a new method is required. If we speak a thought, that thought, while we speak it, must occupy our minds. We could not speak it unless we thought it. By continually repeating "I have no pain" the sufferer constantly renews that thought in his mind. Unfortunately, after each repetition the pain-thought insinuates itself, so that the mind oscillates between "I have no pain" and "I have some pain," or "I have a bad pain." But if we repeat our phrase so rapidly that the contrary association has no time to insert itself, we compel the mind willy-nilly to dwell on it. Thus by a fresh path we reach the same goal as that attained by induced outcropping; we cause an idea to remain in occupation of the mind without calling up a contrary association. This we found to be the prime condition of acceptation, and in fact by this means we can compel the Unconscious to realise the "no-pain" thought and so put an end to the pain.

But the sentence "I have no pain" does not lend itself to rapid repetition. The physical difficulties are too great; the tongue and lips become entangled in the syllables and we have to stop to restore order. Even if we were dexterous enough to articulate the words successfully, we should only meet with a new difficulty. The most emphatic word in the phrase is "pain"; involuntarily we should find ourself stressing this word with particular force, so strengthening in our minds the very idea we are trying to dislodge.

We shall do best to copy as closely as we can Coué's own procedure. The phrase he uses, "ça passe," makes no mention of the hurt; it is extremely easy to say, and it produces an unbroken stream of sound, like the whirr of a machine or the magnified buzz of an insect, which, as it were, carries the mind off its feet. The phrase recommended by Baudouin, "It is passing off," produces no such effect, and in fact defies all our attempts to repeat it quickly. On the whole, the most suitable English version seems to be "It's going." Only the word "going" should be repeated, and the treatment should conclude with the emphatic statement "gone!" The word "going," rapidly gabbled, gives the impression of a mechanical drill, biting its way irresistibly into some hard substance. We can think of it as drilling the desired thought into the mind.

If you are suffering from any severe pain, such as toothache or headache, sit down, close your eyes and assure yourself calmly that you are going to get rid of it. Now gently stroke with your hand the affected part and repeat at the same time as fast as you can, producing a continuous stream of sound, the words: "It's going, going, going . . . gone!" Keep it up for about a minute, pausing only to take a deep breath when necessary, and using the word " gone " only at the conclusion of the whole proceeding. At the end of this time the pain will either have entirely ceased or at least sensibly abated. In either case apply the particular suggestions recommended in the previous chapter. If the pain has ceased suggest that it will not return; if it has only diminished suggest that it will shortly pass away altogether. Now return to whatever employment you were engaged in when the pain began. Let other interests occupy your attention. If in a reasonable space, say half an hour, the pain still troubles you, isolate yourself again; suggest once more that you are going to master it, and repeat the procedure.

It is no exaggeration to say that by this process any pain can be conquered. It may be, in extreme cases, that you will have to return several times to the attack. This will generally occur when you have been foolish enough to supply the pain with a cause—a decayed tooth, a draught of cold air, etc.—and so justify it to your reason, and give it, so to speak, an intellectual sanction. Or it may be that it will cease only to return again. But do not be discouraged; attack it firmly and you are bound to succeed.

The same procedure is equally effective with distressing states of mind, worry, fear, despondency. In such cases the stroking movement of the hand should be applied to the forehead.

Even in this exercise no more effort should be used than is necessary. Simply repeat rapidly the word which informs you that the trouble is going, and let this, with the stroking movement of the hand, which, as it were, fixes the attention to that particular spot, be the sum and substance of your effort. With practice it will become easier, you will "drop into it"; that is to say, the Unconscious will perform the adaptations necessary to make it more effective. After a time you should be able to obtain relief in twenty to twenty-five seconds. But the effect is still more far-reaching; you will be delivered from the fear of pain. Regarding yourself as its master, you will be able with the mere threat of treatment to prevent it from developing. You will hang up a card, "No admittance," on the doors of your conscious mind.

It may be that the pain attacks you in the street or in a workshop; in some public place where the audible repetition of the phrase would attract attention. In that case it is best to close the eyes for a moment and formulate this particular suggestion: "I shall not add to this trouble by thinking about it; my mind will be occupied by other things; but on the first opportunity I shall make it pass away." Then as soon as you can conveniently do so make use of the phrase "It's going." When you have become expert in the use of this form of suggestion you will be able to exorcise the trouble by repeating the phrase mentally—at any rate if the words are outlined with the lips and tongue. But the beginner should rely for a time entirely on audible treatment. By dropping it too soon he will only court disappointment.

It sometimes happens that a patient is so prostrated by pain or misery that he has not the energy to undertake even the repetition of the word "going." The pain-thought so obsesses the mind that the state of painlessness seems too remote even to contemplate. Under these circumstances it seems best to employ this strategy. Lie down on a bed, sofa, or arm-chair and relax both mind and body. Cease from all effort—

which can only make things worse—and let the pain-thought have its way. After a time your energies will begin to collect themselves, your mind to reassert its control. Now make a firm suggestion of success and apply the method. Get another person to help you, as Coué helps his patients, by performing the passes with the hand and repeating the phrase with you. By this means you can make quite sure of success. This seemingly contradictory proceeding is analogous to that of the angler " playing " a fish. He waits till it has run its course before bringing his positive resources into play.

Baudouin recommends an analogous proceeding as a weapon against insomnia. The patient, he says, should rapidly repeat the phrase, " I am going to sleep," letting his mind be swept away by a torrent of words. Once more the objection arises that the phrase " I am going to sleep " is not such as we *can* rapidly repeat. But even if we substitute for it some simple phrase which can be easily articulated it is doubtful whether it will succeed in more than a small percentage of cases. Success is more likely to attend us if we avail ourselves of the method of reflective repetition mentioned in the last chapter. We should take up the position most favourable to slumber and then repeat slowly and contemplatively the word " Sleep." The more impersonal our attitude towards the idea the more rapidly it will be realised in our own slumbers.

## CHAPTER X

## AUTOSUGGESTION AND THE CHILD

IN treating children it should be remembered that autosuggestion is primarily not a remedy but a means of insuring healthy growth. It should not be reserved for times when the child is sick, but provided daily, with the same regularity as meals.

Children grow up weakly not from lack of energy, but because of a waste and misapplication of it. The inner conflict, necessitated by the continual process of adaptation which we call growth, is often of quite unnecessary violence, not only making a great temporary demand on the child's vital energy, but even locking it up in the Unconscious in the form of " complexes," so that its future life is deprived of a portion of its due vitality. A wise use of autosuggestion will preclude these disasters. Growth will be ordered and controlled. The necessary conflicts will be brought to a successful issue, the unnecessary ones avoided.

Autosuggestion may very well begin *before* the child is born. It is a matter of common knowledge that a mother must be shielded during pregnancy from any experience involving shock or fright, since these exert a harmful effect on the developing embryo, and may in extreme cases result in abortion, or in physical deformity or mental weakness in the child. Instances of this ill-effect are comparatively common, and the link between cause and effect is often unmistakable. There is no need to point out that these cases are nothing more than spontaneous autosuggestions operating in the maternal Unconscious; since during pregnancy the mother moulds her little one not only by the food she eats but also by the thoughts she thinks. The heightened emotionality characteristic of this state bespeaks an increased tendency to outcropping, and so an increased suggestibility. Thus spontaneous autosuggestions are far more potent than in the normal course of life. But, happily, induced autosuggestions are aided by the same conditions, so that the mother awake to her powers and duties can do as much good as the ignorant may do harm.

Without going into debatable questions, such as the possibility of predetermining the sex of the child to be born, one can find many helpful ways of aiding and benefiting the growing life by autosuggestive means. The mother should avoid with more than ordinary care all subjects, whether in reading or conversation, which bear on evil in any form, and she should seek whatever uplifts the mind and furnishes it with beautiful and joyous thought. But the technical methods of autosuggestion can also be brought into action.

The mother should suggest to herself that her organism is furnishing the growing life with all it needs, and that the child will be strong and healthy in mind, in body, and in character.

These suggestions should be in general terms bearing on qualities of undoubted good, for obviously it is not desirable to define an independent life too narrowly. They need consist only of a few sentences, and should be formulated night and morning immediately before or after the general formula. Furthermore, when the mother's thoughts during the day stray to the subject of her child, she can take this opportunity to repeat the whole or some part of the particular suggestion she has chosen. These few simple measures will amply suffice. Any undue tendency of the mind to dwell on the thought of the child, even in the form of good suggestions, should not be encouraged. A normal mental life is in itself the best of conditions for the welfare of both mother and child. For her own sake however the mother might well suggest that the delivery will be painless and easy.

The only direct means of autosuggestion applicable to the child for some months after birth is that of the caress, though it must be remembered that the mental states of mother and nurse are already stamping themselves on the little mind, forming it inevitably for better or worse. Should any specific trouble arise, the method of Mlle. Kauffmant should be applied by the mother. Taking the child on her knee she should gently caress the affected part, thinking the while of its reinstatement in perfect health. It seems generally advisable to express these thoughts in words. Obviously, the words themselves will mean nothing to an infant of two or three months, but they will hold the mother's thought in the right channel, and this thought, by the tone of her voice, the touch of her hand, will be communicated to the child. Whether telepathy plays any part in this process we need not inquire, but the baby is psychically as well as physically so dependent on the mother that her mental states are communicated by means quite ineffective with adults. Love in itself exerts a suggestive power of the highest order.

When the child shows signs of understanding what is said to it, before it begins itself to speak, the following method should be applied. After the little one has fallen asleep at night the mother enters the room, taking care not to awaken it, and stands about a yard from the head of the cot. She proceeds then to formulate in a whisper such suggestions as seem necessary. If the child is ailing the suggestion might take the form of the phrase " You are getting better " repeated twenty times. If it is in health the general formula will suffice. Particular suggestions may also be formulated bearing on the child's health, character, intellectual development, etc. These of course should be in accordance with the instructions given in the chapter devoted to particular suggestions. On withdrawing, the mother should again be careful not to awaken the little one. Should it show signs of waking, the whispered command " sleep," repeated several times, will lull it again to rest. Baudouin recommends that during these suggestions the mother should lay her hand on the child's forehead. The above, however, is the method preferred by Coué.

This nightly practice is the most effective means of conveying autosuggestions to the child-mind. It should be made a regular habit which nothing is allowed to interrupt. If for any reason the mother is unable to perform it, her place may be taken by the father, the nurse, or some relative. But for obvious reasons the duty belongs by right to the mother, and, when a few weeks' practice has revealed its beneficent power, few mothers will be willing to delegate it to a less suitable agent.

This practice, as stated above, may well begin before the child has actually learned to speak, for its Unconscious will already be forming a scheme more or less distinct of the significance of the sounds that reach it, and will not fail to gather the general tenor of the words spoken. The date at which it should be discontinued is less easy to specify. Growth, to be healthy, must carry with it a gradual increase in independence and self-sufficiency. There seems to be some slight danger that the practice of nightly suggestions, if continued too long, might prolong unduly the state of dependence upon parental support. Reliable indications on this point are furnished, however, by the child itself. As soon as it is able to face its daily problems for itself, when it no longer runs to the parent for help and advice in every little difficulty, the time will have arrived for the parental suggestions to cease.

As soon as a child is able to speak it should be taught to repeat the general formula night and morning in the same way as an adult. Thus when the time comes to discontinue the parent's suggestions their effect will be carried on by those the child formulates itself. There is one thing more to add: in the case of boys it would seem better at the age of seven or eight for the father to replace the mother in the rôle of suggester, while the mother, of course, performs the office throughout for her girls. Should any signs appear that the period of puberty is bringing with it undue difficulties or perils, the nightly practice might be resumed in the form of particular suggestions bearing on the specific difficulties. It must be remembered, however, that the child's sexual problem is essentially different from that of the adult, and the suggestions must therefore be in the most general terms. Here as elsewhere the end alone should be suggested, the Unconscious being left free to choose its own means.

As soon as the child has learnt to speak it should not be allowed to suffer pain. The best method to adopt is that practised by Coué in his consultations.

Let the child close its eyes and repeat with the parent, "It's going, going . . . gone!" while the latter gently strokes the affected part. But as soon as possible the child should be encouraged to overcome smaller difficulties for itself, until the parent's help is eventually almost dispensed with. This is a powerful means of developing self-reliance and fostering the sense of superiority to difficulties which will be invaluable in later life.

That children readily take to the practice is shown by these examples, which are again quoted from letters received by Coué.

"Your youngest disciple is our little David. The poor little chap had an accident to-day. Going up in the lift with his father, when quite four feet up, he fell out on his head and on to a hard stone floor. He was badly bruised and shocked, and when put to bed lay still and kept saying: 'ça passe, ça passe,' over and over again, and then looked up and said, 'no, not gone away.' To-night he said again 'ça passe' and then added, 'nearly gone.' So he is better."

B. K. (London).

8 *January,* 1922.

Another lady writes:

"Our cook's little niece, aged 23 months—the one we cured of bronchitis—gave herself a horrid blow on the head yesterday. Instead of crying she began to smile, passed her hand over the place and said sweetly, 'ça passe.' Hasn't she been well brought up?"

All these methods are extremely simple and involve little expenditure of time and none of money. They have proved their efficacy over and over again in

Nancy, and there is no reason why a mother of average intelligence and conscientiousness should not obtain equally good results. Naturally, first attempts will be a little awkward, but there is no need for discouragement on that account. Even supposing that through the introduction of effort some slight harm were done—and the chance is comparatively remote—this need cause no alarm. The right autosuggestion will soon counteract it and produce positive good in its place. But any mother who has practised autosuggestion for herself will be able correctly to apply it to her child.

At first glance the procedure may seem revolutionary, but think it over for a moment and you will see that it is as old as the hills. It is merely a systematisation on a scientific basis of the method mothers have intuitively practised since the world began. " Sleep, baby, sleep. Angels are watching o'er thee,"—what is this but a particular suggestion? How does a wise mother proceed when her little one falls and grazes its hand? She says something of this kind: " Let me kiss it and then it will be well." She kisses it, and with her assurance that the pain has gone the child runs happily back to its play. This is only a charming variation of the method of the caress.

# CHAPTER XI

## CONCLUSION

INDUCED Autosuggestion is not a substitute for medical practice. It will not make us live for ever, neither will it free us completely from the common ills of life. What it may do in the future, when all its implications have been realised, all its resources exploited, we cannot say. There is no doubt that a generation brought up by its canons would differ profoundly from the disease-ridden population of to-day. But our immediate interest is with the present.

The adult of to-day carries in his Unconscious a memory clogged with a mass of adverse suggestions which have been accumulating since childhood. The first task of Induced Autosuggestion will be to clear away this mass of mental lumber. Not until this has been accomplished can the real man appear and the creative powers of autosuggestion begin to manifest themselves.

By the use of this method each one of us should be able to look forward to a life in which disease is a diminishing factor. But how great a part it will play depends upon the conditions we start from and the regularity and correctness of our practice. Should disease befall us we possess within a potent means of expelling it, but this does not invalidate the complementary method of destroying it from without. Autosuggestion and the usual medical practice should go hand in hand, each supplementing the other. If you are ill, call in your doctor as before, but enlist the resources of Induced Autosuggestion to reinforce and extend his treatment.

In this connection it must be insisted on that autosuggestion should be utilised for every ailment, whatever its nature, and whether its inroads be grave or slight. Every disease is either strengthened or weakened by the action of the mind. We cannot take up an attitude of neutrality. Either we must aid the disease to destroy us by allowing our minds to dwell on it, or we must oppose it and destroy it by a stream of healthful dynamic thought. Too frequently we spontaneously adopt the former course.

The general opinion that functional and nervous diseases alone are susceptible to suggestive treatment is at variance with the facts. During Coué's thirty years of practice, in which many thousands of cases have been treated, he has found that organic troubles yield as easily as functional, that bodily derangements are even easier to cure than nervous and mental. He makes no such distinctions; an illness is an illness whatever its nature. As such Coué attacks it, and in 98 per cent. of cases he attains in greater or less degree a positive result.

Apart from the permanently insane, in whose minds the machinery of autosuggestion is itself deranged, there are only two classes of patient with whom Induced Autosuggestion seems to fail. One consists of persons whose intelligence is so low that the directions given are never comprehended; the other of those who lack the power of voluntary attention and cannot devote their minds to an idea even for a few consecutive seconds. These two classes, however, are numerically insignificant, together making up not much more than 2 per cent. of the population.

Autosuggestion is equally valuable as an aid to surgical practice. A broken bone—the sceptic's last resource—cannot of course be treated by autosuggestion alone. A surgeon must be called in to mend it. But when the limb has been rightly set and the necessary mechanical precautions have been taken, autosuggestion will provide the best possible conditions for recovery. It can prevent lameness, stiffness, unsightly deformity and the other evils which a broken limb is apt to entail, and it will shorten considerably the normal period of convalescence.

It is sometimes stated that the results obtained by autosuggestion are not permanent. This objection is really artificial, arising from the fact that we ignore the true nature of autosuggestion and regard it merely as a remedy. When we employ autosuggestion to heal a malady our aim is so to leaven the Unconscious with healthful thoughts, that not only will that specific malady be excluded, but all others with it. Autosuggestion should not only remove a particular form of disease, but the tendency to all disease.

If after an ailment has been removed we allow our mind to revert to unhealthy thoughts, they will tend to realise themselves in the same way as any others, and we may again fall a victim to ill-health. Our sickness may take the same form as on the preceding occasion, or it may not. That will depend on the nature of our thought. But by the regular employment of the general formula we can prevent any such recurrence. Instead of reverting to unhealthy states of mind we shall progressively strengthen the healthy and creative thought that has already given us health, so that with each succeeding day our defence will be more impenetrable. Not only do we thus avoid a relapse into former ailments but we clear out of our path those which lie in wait for us in the future.

We saw that in the Nancy clinic some of the cures effected are almost instantaneous. It would be a mistake, however, to embark on the practice of Induced Autosuggestion with the impression that we are going to be miraculously healed in the space of a few days. Granted sufficient faith, such a result would undoubtedly ensue; nay, more, we have records of quite a number of such cases, even where the help of a second person has not been called in. Here is an example. A friend of mine, M. Albert P., of Bordeaux, had suffered for more than ten years with neuralgia of the face. Hearing of Coué, he wrote to him, and received instructions to repeat the general formula. He did so, and on the second day the neuralgia had vanished and has never since returned. But such faith is not common. Immediate cures are the exception, and it will be safer for us to look forward to a gradual and progressive improvement. In this way we shall guard against disappointment. It may be added that Coué prefers the gradual cure, finding it more stable and less likely to be disturbed by adverse conditions.

We should approach autosuggestion in the same reasonable manner as we approach any other scientific discovery. There is no hocus-pocus about it, nor are any statements made here which experience cannot verify. But the attitude we should beware most of is that of the intellectual amateur, who makes the vital things of life small coin to exchange with his neighbour of the dinner-table. Like religion, autosuggestion is a thing to practise. A man may be conversant with all the creeds in Christendom and be none the better for it; while some simple soul, loving God and his fellows, may combine the high principles of Christianity in his life without any acquaintance with theology. So it is with autosuggestion.

Autosuggestion is just as effective in the treatment of moral delinquencies as in that of physical ills. Drunkenness, kleptomania, the drug habit, uncontrolled or perverted sexual desires, as well as minor failings of character, are all susceptible to its action. It is as powerful in small things as in great. By particular suggestions we can modify our tastes. We can acquire a relish for the dishes we naturally dislike, and make disagreeable medicine taste pleasant. So encouraging has been its application to the field of morals that Coué is trying to gain admittance to the French state reformatories. So far, the official dislike for innovations has proved a barrier, but there is good reason to hope that in the near future the application of this method to the treatment of the criminal will be greatly extended.

By way of anticipating an objection it may be stated that the Coué method of Induced Autosuggestion is in no sense inferior to hypnotic suggestion. Coué himself began his career as a hypnotist, but being dissatisfied with the results, set out in quest of a method more simple and universal. Conscious autosuggestion, apart from its convenience, can boast one great advantage over its rival. The effects of hypnotic suggestion are often lost within a few hours of the treatment. Whereas by the use of the general formula the results of Induced Autosuggestion go on progressively augmenting.

Here we touch again the question of the suggester.

We have already seen that a suggester is not needed, that autosuggestion can yield its fullest fruits to those who practise it unaided. But some persons cannot be prevailed on to accept this fact. They feel a sense of insufficiency; the mass of old wrong suggestions has risen so mountain-high that they imagine themselves incapable of removing it. With such the presence of a suggester is an undoubted help. They have nothing to do but lie passive and receive the ideas he evokes. Even so, however, they will get little good unless they consent to repeat the general formula.

But as long as we look on autosuggestion as a remedy we miss its true significance. Primarily it is a means of self-culture, and one far more potent than any we have hitherto possessed. It enables us to develop the mental qualities we lack: efficiency, judgment, creative imagination, all that will help us to bring our life's enterprise to a successful end. Most of us are aware of thwarted abilities, powers undeveloped, impulses checked in their growth. These are present in our Unconscious like trees in a forest, which, overshadowed by their neighbours, are stunted for lack of air and sunshine. By means of autosuggestion we can supply them with the power needed for growth and bring them to fruition in our conscious lives. However old, however infirm, however selfish, weak or vicious we may be, autosuggestion will do something for us. It gives us a new means of culture and discipline by which the " accents immature," the " purposes unsure " can be nursed into strength, and the evil impulses attacked at the root. It is essentially an individual practice, an individual attitude of mind. Only a narrow view would split it up into categories, debating its application to this thing or to that. It touches our being in its wholeness. Below the fussy perturbed little ego, with its local habitation, its name, its habits and views and oddities is an ocean of power, as serene as the depths below the troubled surface of the sea. Whatever is of you comes eventually thence, however perverted by the prism of self-consciousness. Autosuggestion is a channel by which the tranquil powers of this ultimate being are raised to the level of our life here and now.

What prospects does autosuggestion open to us in the future?

It teaches us that the burdens of life are, at least in large measure, of our own creating. We reproduce in ourselves and in our circumstances the thoughts of our minds. It goes further. It offers us a means by which we can change these thoughts when they are evil and foster them when they are good, so producing a corresponding betterment in our individual life. But the process does not end with the individual. The thoughts of society are realised in social conditions, the thoughts of humanity in world conditions. What would be the attitude towards our social and international problems of a generation nurtured from infancy in the knowledge and practice of autosuggestion? If fear and disease were banned from the individual life, could they persist in the life of the nation? If each person found happiness in his own heart would the illusory greed for possession survive? The acceptance of autosuggestion entails a change of attitude, a re-valuation of life. If we stand with our faces westward we see nothing but clouds and darkness, yet by a simple turn of the head we bring the wide panorama of the sunrise into view.

That Coué's discoveries may profoundly affect our

educational methods is beyond question. Hitherto we have been dealing directly only with the conscious mind, feeding it with information, grafting on to it useful accomplishments. What has been done for the development of character has been incidental and secondary. This was inevitable so long as the Unconscious remained undiscovered, but now we have the means of reaching profounder depths, of endowing the child not only with reading and arithmetic, but with health, character and personality.

But perhaps it is in our treatment of the criminal that the greatest revolution may be expected. The acts for which he is immured result from nothing more than twists and tangles of the threads of thought in the Unconscious mind. This is the view of eminent authorities. But autosuggestion takes us a long step further. It shows how these discords of character may be resolved. Since Coué has succeeded in restoring to moral health a youth of homicidal tendencies, why should not the same method succeed with many of the outcasts who fill our prisons? At least the younger delinquents should prove susceptible. But the idea underlying this attitude entails a revolution in our penal procedure. It means little less than this: that crime is a disease and should be treated as such; that the idea of punishment must give place to that of cure; the vindictive attitude to one of pity. This brings us near to the ideals of the New Testament, and indeed, autosuggestion, as a force making for goodness, is bound to touch closely on religion.

It teaches the doctrine of the inner life which saints and sages have proclaimed through all ages. It asserts that within are the sources of calm, of power and of courage, and that the man who has once attained mastery of this inner sphere is secure in the face of all that may befall him. This truth is apparent in the lives of great men. Martyrs could sing at the stake because their eyes were turned within on the vision of glory which filled their hearts. Great achievements have been wrought by men who had the fortitude to follow the directions of an inner voice, even in contradiction to the massed voices they heard without.

Suppose we find that the power Christ gave to his disciples to work miracles of healing was not a gift conferred on a few selected individuals, but was the heritage of all men; that the kingdom of heaven within us to which He alluded was available in a simple way for the purging and elevation of our common life, for procuring sounder health and sweeter minds. Is not the affirmation contained in Coué's formula a kind of prayer? Does it not appeal to something beyond the self-life, to the infinite power lying behind us?

Autosuggestion is no substitute for religion; it is rather a new weapon added to the religious armoury. If as a mere scientific technique it can yield such results, what might it not do as the expression of those high yearnings for perfection which religion incorporates?

Printed in the United States
113917LV00001B/159-176/A